REVOLUTION
WITHIN THE REVOLUTION

REVOLUTION
WITHIN THE
REVOLUTION

*The First Amendment in
Historical Context, 1612–1789*

William R. Estep

WILLIAM B. EERDMANS PUBLISHING COMPANY
GRAND RAPIDS, MICHIGAN

Copyright © 1990 by Wm. B. Eerdmans Publishing Co.
255 Jefferson Ave. S.E., Grand Rapids, Mich. 49503

Printed in the United States of America

Library of Congress Cataloging-in-Publication Data

Estep, William Roscoe, 1920-
The revolution within the Revolution: the First Amendment in historical
context, 1612-1789 / William R. Estep.
p.   cm.
Includes bibliographical references.
ISBN 0-8028-0458-6
1. Freedom of religion—United States—History.   2. Religion and
state—United States—History.   3. United States—Religion   4. Church and
state—United States—History.   5. United
States—Constitution—Amendments—1st.   I. Title.
BR516.E886   1990
323.44′2′0973—dc20   90-35775
                                                      CIP

To
the memory of my mother

Rhoda Snyder Estep

Exemplary Christian and Political Activist

Contents

Foreword

Recently, I broadcast on public television a documentary called "The Battle for the Bible," detailing the efforts by one faction within the Southern Baptist Convention—America's largest Protestant denomination—to establish the inerrancy of the Bible as a theological litmus test for membership in the faith. Biblical inerrancy has been defined as "a creed of compulsory affirmation that the Bible is always perfectly clear and is true in every detail, whether the detail is a matter of history, science or religion." Its adherents have waged a decade-long crusade to take over the agencies, schools, and seminaries and enforce acceptance of their doctrine. Not the Bible itself but beliefs about the Bible would become the source of Baptist theology—that has been the avowed goal. The ultimate aim, however, has been not theological but political. Through an intricate network of public and private alliances, the leaders of the inerrancy faction have committed themselves to a partisan strategy of collusion between church and state that also makes a mockery of the historic Baptist principles of religious liberty.

It is an astonishing development largely untold by the mainstream press. Religious folk have long pressed their moral values on the body politic, but this new hierarchy of Southern Baptists has gone beyond advocacy and persuasion to seek a privileged relationship with the government. While others—

Catholics, Lutherans, and Anglicans, for instance—have through the centuries sought the status of an established religion, this is a radical departure for Baptists. Just as revolutionary is the attempt by these leaders to keep the laity generally unaware of what is being done in their name or to their principles. Historically Baptist ministers have been primarily preachers and pastors, accountable to the democratic polity of their local congregations; they have not sought a priestly role or served as precinct captains. But in recent years, certain Baptist clergy and certain politically ambitious laymen have been making back-room deals with right-wing politicians, permitting White House operatives to draft resolutions which have then been submitted—their origin unidentified—to official Baptist assemblies, and waging guerrilla war against their own brothers and sisters in the faith. In the course of reporting for the documentary, my colleagues and I uncovered direct links between the principal movers of the inerrantist faction and right-wing organizers, funders, and strategists, with patronage plums being handed out in return for favors rendered. The chief architect of the crusade was himself scheduled for a top presidential appointment until the required background check turned up allegations of behavior that would have been embarrassing at his Senate confirmation hearings, and the proposed nomination was dropped. This individual remains close to the White House, however, and continues to dominate the inner circle of men who now control the Southern Baptist Convention. Under their influence, the role of the clergy has taken an increasingly authoritarian turn, and notions of theocracy have been sounded where once they would have shocked.

For many of us who were raised in the tradition, these developments betray our heritage in at least two ways. First, Baptists have prided themselves on their belief that the individual believer has a personal and dynamic relationship with God, one that does not need the intermediary of a clergy or a hierarchy or, least of all, an official interpretation of Scripture. Ever since the Baptists of England pleaded with James I for freedom of conscience, Baptist historical struggles against established churches have been not so much against particular beliefs as against imposed *ways* of believing. Foremost among Baptist convictions—the reason for so much of the dissent that has marked Baptist history—is the right of the individual to follow the dictates of his or her conscience, free from the oppression of an overarching authority, secular or ecclesiastical. Furthermore, every Baptist church is a self-governing democracy; mandates on matters of politics and morals do not come down to local congregations. What has happened over the past decade amounts to no less than the hijacking of this tradition. The leaders of the inerrancy faction have erected a gate through which must pass all those who call themselves Baptist. The gatekeepers will then certify everyone who passes muster, and reject those who do not. An ecclesiastical politburo has staged a coup of the Baptist faith and has declared heretical any who challenge the new orthodoxy of conformity.

Second, by marrying the Republican right, the inerrancy faction has declared war on Baptists' unique contribution to the American Idea. Historically Baptists have abhorred the mere hint of theocracy. It was a Baptist, after all, who founded the civil commonwealth called the Providence Plantations. Roger Williams had been hounded from the colony of Massachusetts for his espousal of conscience. Under his inspiration—and then the leadership of Dr. John Clarke, pastor of the Baptist Church of Newport—Rhode Island became the first colony with a civil government through which full religious liberty was guaranteed to all its inhabitants. Baptists then helped to shape the struggle of the colonies for independence and the spiritual foundations of the new republic with their insistence that Caesar's coin corrupts. They knew it would lead to increased sectarian strife, purchased favoritism, and entangling alliances—all at the expense of the freedom of the soul. Experience taught them these lessons, for in the colony of Virginia alone, between 1767 and 1778, over forty Baptist ministers were slapped in jail for defying the established church, which was backed by the coercive power of the state.

The book you hold in your hands is a timely reminder of such things. William Estep has steeped his adult life in Baptist history and Baptist principles. I was one of his students many years ago at Southwestern Baptist Theological Seminary. His scholarly passion in the classroom echoes in these pages. So does that deep love for liberty which is the bedrock of Baptist belief in the separation of church and state.

The core of Dr. Estep's argument is this: "In an increasingly intolerant age, it is well for us to retrace the painful steps of those who first discovered in the gospel the demand for an uncoerced faith and articulated their insights with incredible courage." He sets this history against an analysis which sees many Baptists today confused by events in the modern world and within their own ranks, so that, knowingly or not, they often repudiate their own heritage. (He cites one prominent Southern Baptist minister, to wit: "I believe the notion of the separation of church and state was the figment of some infidel's imagination.") The task he sets himself is to retell the Baptist story with such clarity that the confusion will be routed and Baptists will recover the sharp edge of their witness to liberty.

But this book is not just a primer for Baptists. As Dr. Estep points out, the collusion between the new Southern Baptist hierarchy and partisan political power also threatens the First Amendment, for it undermines the notion that individuals are to be defended against the depredations of such collusion. The desire to create a civil religion, a state-sanctioned web of religious beliefs, can only, in his words, "reduce the Almighty to a national icon . . . [and make Christianity] little more than cheap nationalism."

Again, early Baptists foresaw this danger. Dr. Estep reminds us, for example, that the First Amendment had no advocate more ardent than John Leland, the Baptist minister who, with other lovers of liberty, pressured James Madison for a constitutional amendment on religious liberty. They had scrutinized the proposed Constitution and found it wanting. The First Amendment was their asking price for supporting the new charter. As Leland and others argued, a government which arrogated to itself the task of compelling the faith of its citizens would inevitably impose an orthodoxy on people that would stifle their consciences and cause rebellion. In the same way, a religion which relied on the state to discipline the behavior of believers would soon corrupt its own beliefs and encourage hypocrisy. Only if church and state were true to their own unique natures could they govern their proper worlds well: "actions only and not opinions" for government, as Jefferson wrote, and the "priesthood of the individual believer" for religion.

Thus, two hundred years later, the takeover of the Southern Baptist Convention by absolutists seeking privilege from the state is no intramural dispute, no little cloud on the periphery of public affairs. The battle for the Bible is a test of our democracy's commitment to its basic guarantees of freedom. In such an hour, we need a strong reminder and an accurate record of the tradition that is endangered and of the consequences should it be lost. William Estep courageously has provided us both reminder and record, and we are in his debt.

BILL MOYERS

Acknowledgments

This book has been in the process of development for a number of years. Therefore, I am indebted to many scholars whose painstaking research has made my task much easier. Upon occasion I have dared to differ with authors whose conclusions, in my opinion, were not warranted by the evidence. But to those with whom I have disagreed I also owe a debt of gratitude, for they have challenged me to think through my own presuppositions and conclusions. Unfortunately, I am not able to indicate my indebtedness in every case, for even I am not aware of ideas which were borrowed from others long ago. However, I do wish to express my gratitude to many without whom this book could not have taken shape.

First, some of the material in this work may sound familiar to those students and faculty members before whom I have presented papers or given lectures in recent years. The schools at which I have spoken include Fresno Pacific College, Fresno, California; Cumberland College, Williamsburg, Kentucky; Bethel College, North Newton, Kansas; Wheaton College, Wheaton, Illinois; Abilene Christian University, Abilene, Texas; Baylor University, Waco, Texas; Phillips University, Enid, Oklahoma; and Tulsa University, Tulsa, Oklahoma. Of course, my students at Southwestern Baptist Theological Seminary have provided a captive audience for many of the concepts which reverberate through the pages of this book.

Many libraries have extended courtesies to me for which I will always be grateful. Among these are the Bodleian Library, the Library of Congress, the Mary Couts Burnett Library at Texas Christian University, and the A. Webb Roberts Library at Southwestern. A special word of thanks is due Mr. Robert Philips, Assistant Director of the A. Webb Roberts Library, for his gracious assistance upon numerous occasions. I am also indebted to Dr. Fred Anderson, Executive Director of the Virginia Baptist Historical Society, who has provided copies of rare prison documents which are included in the Appendix.

I am grateful for the foreword to this volume written by Bill Moyers. At one time, he was one of my students, but in recent years I have become his student, as have the multiplied millions who have viewed his informative and challenging television presentations.

Three colleagues have taken time to read my manuscript in an early stage of preparation and have made a number of valuable suggestions for its improvement. These include Professor Robert A. Baker, my mentor and colleague in the Church History Department at Southwestern for some twenty-six years; Professor Ronald B. Flowers, Associate Professor of Religion at Texas Christian University and co-author of *Toward Benevolent Neutrality: Church, State, and the Supreme Court*; and Professor John P. Newport, a friend of many years and Academic Vice-President and Provost of Southwestern.

I also wish to express my appreciation to those who have actually helped to prepare the manuscript for publication. Miss Susan Day, a Master of Divinity graduate at Southwestern, typed the manuscript and prepared the index. Mr. Stephen Stookey, a Ph.D. student in church history at Southwestern, has aided me in proofreading the appendix and bibliography. To Ms. Mary Hietbrink, who edited this book for Eerdmans and by her editorial skills made it a better book than would otherwise have been the case, I wish to say "Thank you."

Acknowledgments

A special word of appreciation is due my wife, Edna, without whose help in so many ways, beyond computation, none of my books could have been written.

Fort Worth, Texas
March 15, 1990

Preface

What made the United States of America unique among the nations of the world in 1789 were the constitutional provisions for the separation of church and state. The First Amendment provided a guarantee of religious liberty that didn't exist in any other country. Two hundred years have passed since its enactment by the congress of the infant republic. Since then, pluralism has become a way of life in matters religious in the United States. As a result, Christianity and Judaism have flourished here as in no other country, and the United States has been relatively free of violence provoked by religious strife. For this state of religious affairs we have a revolution within the Revolution to thank.

In an increasingly intolerant age, it is good for us to retrace the painful steps of those who first discovered in the gospel the demand for an uncoerced faith and articulated their insights with incredible courage. Accordingly, this work examines more than the crucial decade that brought religious freedom to Virginia. The historical process of which the First Amendment was the climactic event is traced back to England and the Continent to the despised progenitors of the Free Church movement, the Anabaptists and English Separatists of the sixteenth and the seventeenth centuries.

It was the English-speaking world which saw the seeds of

religious freedom that were first sown by the "heretics" sprout and eventually burst into full bloom. Although the English Separatists paid a heavy price for their nonconformity, the Act of Toleration of 1689, with all its limitations, was their only trophy in the end—or was it? What survived one purge after another were the tracts and confessions of faith in which they set forth their arguments for freedom, arguments underlined by their imprisonment and martyrdom. These little pamphlets, often poorly written and carelessly printed, provided a bridge of ideas from Old England to the English colonies of the New World. But it took more than ideas to bring to life religious freedom in the American experience—it took action.

God acted—as those involved fervently believed—in the Great Awakening. And God-intoxicated individuals acted to bring about a revolution within the Revolution. For these dissenters the struggle for religious freedom became the means by which they became patriots. Isaac Backus, agent of the Warren Association; John Gano, Washington's chaplain; James Manning, president of Rhode Island College; John Leland, itinerant evangelist; and Reuben Ford of the General Committee—for these men religious freedom was never an end in itself. It was simply the means by which the gospel could be freely proclaimed, responded to, and acted on without interference from an established church or an all-encompassing state.

The history that follows in these pages may sound very much like Baptist history, and to some extent it is—but it is also much more than that. It is a quest for the "original intent" of the First Amendment, which does not begin and end with Madison and Jefferson but goes beyond these founding fathers of the nation to the "twice born" who made it possible.

Fort Worth, Texas   W. R. Estep
1990

Chapter I

Under Siege

*"Congress shall make no law respecting an
establishment of religion, or prohibiting the
free exercise thereof."*

This declaration constitutes the no-establishment clause found
in the First Amendment to the Constitution of the United
States. The basic concepts expressed here were present in the
initial form of the amendment when James Madison presented
it to the House on June 7, 1789. After much debate and some
revision, the final form was approved by the entire congress—
first by the House on September 24, then by the Senate on
September 25, 1789. Ratification by the states followed two
years later.

The adoption of the First Amendment represented the
climax of a long and involved process—how long and how
involved few knew then or, for that matter, know now. Of course,
some elements of this process are beyond human calculation,
but such is not the case with the major events in humanity's
long struggle to be free from the forces of tyranny that would
coerce and enslave both mind and soul.

It is incredible that after two hundred years of reaping the
incalculable benefits of the First Amendment, there are Chris-

tians who appear determined to eliminate it, if not by a constitutional convention then by reinterpretation. The present assault on the First Amendment amounts to a siege—a siege based to a large extent upon misunderstanding, misinformation, and/or distortion. Other factors have also contributed to a situation that constitutes nothing less than a crisis of faith in freedom itself.

THE DISSIDENTS

It is no secret that there have been some ardent advocates of various Old World state churches who have never been happy with the American experience. However, the dissidents now constitute a mixed chorus composed of those who for a variety of motives are calling for "a new Reformation" by which they hope to abolish the institutional separation of church and state embodied in the Constitution and the Bill of Rights. The more strident among them are even calling for a constitutional convention, by which they hope to rewrite the basic documents of the American republic. But most are content, at least for the present, to reinterpret the First Amendment.

These revisionists argue that the First Amendment and the Constitution have been misunderstood and misapplied. A common interpretation found in most of their arguments insists, on the basis of "original intent," that the separation of church and state was not implicit in the First Amendment or that the founding fathers never intended the First Amendment to apply to the states. By citing the Northwest Ordinance of 1787 and the fact that Massachusetts did not give up its established church until 1833, these dissidents lay the groundwork for an attempt to call the nation back to its Puritan heritage and impose a religious agenda upon what they perceive to be a decadent society. Their proposed scenario sounds too good to be true—and it is. It is seriously flawed. Just how erroneous the distortions of the past and the perceptions of the present are can only be disclosed by a more thorough discussion.

TRADITIONAL DISSIDENTS

In Europe, from which the colonizers of the New World came, established church systems were the order of the day. The Catholic, Lutheran, Reformed, and Anglican denominations were "the churches." They enjoyed preferred status, economic support, and exclusive privileges at the expense of "the sects." Frequently they were not only favored by the governments of which they were a part, but they also ruled. A classic example is that of Archbishop William Laud, who under Charles I of England became the Archbishop of Canterbury and thus assumed absolute control of the Star Chamber and Court of High Commission. There is no doubt that before he was sent to the Tower, Laud became, as William Haller has written, "the first man in the Kingdom."[1] He is reported to have said that "the religion of Rome and ours is one and the same," and he gave every indication of believing it. As far as the Puritans and Separatists were concerned, he declared, "I will harass them out of the land." At the same time, the queen—Henrietta Maria, daughter of Henry IV of France—was a Roman Catholic. Thus mass was said daily, and Roman Catholic priests visited Whitehall regularly.[2] According to Haller,

> Laud accepted the Anglican conception of society as it came to him by the way of Hooker and Andrewes.* The church was one with the living whole which was the nation. Rulers were responsible to God for their subjects' welfare, a responsibility to be exercised vigorously and in the fear of the Lord. They should rule so as to secure and retain the reverence and loyalty of a united people.[3]

1. Haller, *The Rise of Puritanism* (New York: Harper & Row, 1957), p. 228. For an incisive account of Laud's career, see A. H. Newman, *A Manual of Church History*, vol. 2 (Philadelphia: American Baptist Publication Society, 1931), pp. 283-85.

2. J. P. Kenyon, *The Stuarts: A Study of English Kingship* (London: Collins-Fontana, 1958), pp. 78-79.

*Richard Hooker provided the intellectual basis for Anglicanism in *Of the Laws of Ecclesiastical Polity*; Lancelot Andrewes became the most eloquent defender and pulpiteer of Anglicanism.

3. Haller, *The Rise of Puritanism*, p. 228.

This vision of a united England meant there was no room for religious dissent. Unfortunately, Laud's ideal was transferred to the crown colonies, particularly Virginia and North Carolina, with varying degrees of success.

The Roman Catholic Church never enjoyed the privileged status in the American colonies that it had experienced for centuries in Europe. Maryland, the one colony established by a Catholic—Lord Baltimore (George Calvert)—provided limited toleration for non-Catholics who professed Christianity. In 1692, Maryland was made a royal colony, and the Church of England became the established church. At the time, Roman Catholics comprised only one-third of the colony's inhabitants. Indeed, at the dawn of the Revolution, the Roman Catholic presence in the colonies was hardly visible. But the great waves of Catholic immigration from Europe in the nineteenth century eventually changed the status of the Roman Catholic Church in the United States from that of a relatively insignificant minority to that of a dominant group in some sections of the country, particularly the northeast.

The establishment of parochial schools, seminaries, and colleges created an enormous need for financial support not readily available within Catholic communities—which, of course, led the church to resort to ingenious ways of raising the necessary cash. Public funds were tapped whenever possible. The virtues of Catholic parochial school education were extolled at the expense of public schools in order to elicit support in the form of both student response and financial support from Catholic laity.[4]

At the same time, Irish, Italian, and German Catholics were arriving on the Atlantic seaboard in ever-increasing numbers; the reactionary Pius IX was making things increasingly difficult for the new arrivals. In 1864 he issued the infamous *Syllabus of Errors*, which set the church against democracy and democratic principles and institutions such as freedom of religion, separation of church and state, public schools, and a free

---

4. Winthrop Hudson, *Religion in America* (New York: Macmillan, 1987), p. 229.

press. Six years later, Vatican Council I proclaimed the dogma of papal infallibility. This act further widened the gulf between American Protestants and the Roman Catholic Church.

Given the growing Catholic presence in the United States, coupled with the encyclicals of Pius IX, it is not surprising that a wave of anti-Catholicism swept across the country. By the end of the nineteenth century, Protestants began to feel threatened to a degree unmatched since the Revolutionary War. It is generally conceded that anti-Catholicism in America reached a peak in 1928 during Alfred E. Smith's campaign to be elected president of the United States. The situation was far different thirty-two years later, when John F. Kennedy was elected president of the United States. Although Kennedy was accused of using charges of anti-Catholicism against the opposition, he did promise to uphold religious freedom.

Kennedy's assurances to guard the separation of church and state appeared to demonstrate to many Protestants and others the final Americanization of the Roman Catholic Church. Consequently, the fear that some had entertained before Kennedy's election—that there was a giant Roman Catholic conspiracy to sabotage religious freedom—was largely dispelled. Vatican Council II reinforced this impression. Called by John XXIII "to bring the church up to date," Vatican II succeeded remarkably well in doing exactly that. The schema of the council, *Declaration on Religious Freedom (Dignitatis Humanae Personae)*, published on 7 December 1965, put the church firmly on the side of religious liberty as a divinely bestowed human right and went a long way toward reversing the negative effects of the *Syllabus of Errors.*

But a few decades later there was a fly in this new ecumenical ointment: President Reagan's appointment of an official ambassador to the Vatican, apparently a move to appease the American Catholic hierarchy, was viewed by some as unconstitutional, a clear violation of the First Amendment. However, there are other indications that American Catholic bishops were prepared to live with the concept of the institutional separation of church and state, albeit with certain reservations.

Since the days of the Reformation, the Lutherans attempted to become "the Church" in many lands but succeeded in doing so only in relatively few German-speaking and Scandinavian countries. Those state churches that Lutherans were able to establish frequently became captive to a civil religion which put the state over the church and failed to distinguish between nationalism and Christianity. Thus the church was prostituted for pagan ends, the most deplorable instance of which occurred in Nazi Germany during the Third Reich.

The Lutheran Church's desire for special status, including financial support and recognition, has gone unfulfilled to a large degree in the United States. Although Germans and Scandinavians flocked to the New World in increasing numbers, the Lutherans among them controlled no colony and enjoyed no established status, except in a few communities and states where they constituted a social establishment. The Lutheran Church has been reduced to one of numerous competing confessional bodies, and some Lutherans are discernibly dissatisfied with the American experience. This much is rather evident in Richard John Neuhaus' *Naked Public Square*.[5] However, most Lutherans, like most Catholics, while they have maintained their own parochial schools, have become an integral part of the American experience, including the pluralism characteristic of American society.

Yet the dissatisfaction with the First Amendment and its implications continues to mount. In reaction to the landmark decision by the Supreme Court in *Roe v. Wade* (1973), which legalized abortion on demand, the New Religious Right has become a major force, making a concerted attempt to reform American society and government in keeping with what it perceives to be the Puritan heritage.

5. Neuhaus, *The Naked Public Square* (Grand Rapids: Wm. B. Eerdmans, 1984), pp. 259-64.

THE NEW DISSIDENTS

The New Dissidents provide the most strident voices in this chorus of discontent. They come from a variety of sources, including the Free Churches. Mainly Calvinists of one sort or another, they receive considerable inspiration from John Calvin; consequently, Geneva becomes the model for the new society they envision for a "Christian America." Their rhetoric often reflects a civil religion that "wraps the cross in the American flag" and fails to distinguish nation from church and patriotism from worship. In their endeavors they are unwittingly dangerously close to making Christianity captive to its culture, and while they attempt to use a political party to accomplish their ends, they may instead end up being used by it. The likely result of this new approach is that the God of the universe will be reduced to a tribal deity. Since the vision of the founding fathers of this nation is at variance with that of the dissidents, that vision must be bypassed, reinterpreted, or discarded.

Baptists Against Separation

In his highly acclaimed work entitled *Fundamentalism and American Culture*, George Marsden hesitates to categorize Baptists because of their diversity. But he is on solid historical grounds when he observes, "While patriotic, almost all [in the first half of the nineteenth century] held dogmatically to the ideal of 'separation of church and state.'"[6] From the beginning of the Baptist movement, all major Baptist confessions have contained articles on religious liberty and the separation of church and state; in fact, these are frequently the longest of the articles. Even the Second London Confession (1677-1689), which repeated verbatim much of the Presbyterian Westminster Confession, included an article (XXI) on religious liberty not

---

6. Marsden, *Fundamentalism and American Culture: The Shaping of Twentieth Century Evangelicalism* (New York: Oxford University Press, 1980), p. 134.

found in the Westminster Confession. A long line of shapers of the Baptist heritage—from John Smyth to George W. Truett, pastor of the First Baptist Church of Dallas—have articulated eloquently this feature of the Baptist faith. One of the major goals prompting the formation of the Baptist World Alliance in 1905 was the promotion of religious liberty around the world.[7]

The Baptist Joint Committee on Public Affairs, the Washington-based organization supported by nine Baptist denominational bodies in the United States and Canada, was called into existence for the purpose of representing Baptist concerns regarding religious liberty and the separation of church and state in the nation's capitol. How is it, then, that some prominent Baptist preachers have joined the siege against the First Amendment?

In a recent article, W. W. Finlator, a Baptist minister from North Carolina, offers his answer:

> Like millions of Americans, we Baptists have a slender sense of history. We have forgotten and forsaken our rich heritage. We have traded our birthright for a mess of something else. We have exchanged the fundamentals for fundamentalism. Because we have forgotten that freedom of religion also means freedom from religion, we behold only an enemy in [Madeleine Murray] O'Hair when she opposes religious coercion by the state.[8]

Stan Hastey, formerly of the Baptist Joint Committee, shares much the same opinion as Finlator. In commenting on Pat Robertson (the Baptist television evangelist and erstwhile presidential candidate who pronounced the separation of church and state a "myth"), and Jerry Falwell (who has declared "We are out to change the First Amendment"), Hastey said, "These so-called Baptists betray their heritage, if indeed they know it at all."[9]

One does not have to go far to substantiate Hastey's

---

7. *The Life of Baptists in the Life of the World*, ed. Walter B. Shurden (Nashville: Broadman Press, 1985), p. 115. The address that Truett delivered to the Congress of the Baptist World Alliance in 1939 is reproduced in this volume. In this speech Truett said, "Religious liberty is the nursing mother of all liberty."

8. Finlator, "They're Trying to Make Us Baptists!" *Christian Century*, 6 Apr. 1983, p. 303.

9. Hastey, *Report from the Capitol*, Oct. 1982, p. 8.

allegation. In August 1984 a prominent Southern Baptist pastor featured on *The CBS Evening News* informed the nation, "I believe the notion of the separation of church and state was the figment of some infidel's imagination." Of course, every church historian worth his tenure knows that Baptists from their earliest inception called for the institutional separation of church and state, as the subsequent pages will document. Then why the present discrepancy—the radical break with this historical distinction of the Baptist heritage? Could it be that Baptists have been so busy evangelizing that they have had little energy or time left to teach history to their converts? Or is it possible that they, too, have succumbed to panic in the face of the avalanche of immorality that threatens to inundate us all? Or have too many listened too long to those with a "takeover mentality," whose only answer appears to be rooted not in the gospel but in "law" and the force of law? At any rate, many contemporary Baptists appear to be confused, with no clear notion of who they are amidst the pied pipers of the New Right.

The Heirs of Luther and Calvin

The heirs of Luther and Calvin suffer no such identity crisis as that which now afflicts the Baptists, who are also indirectly heirs of both Luther and Calvin. True to the state-church concepts of their ecclesiastical forefathers, some within the Lutheran and Reformed traditions are attempting to rewrite the history of the nation. Two individuals are fairly representative of these unhappy dissidents. The first is Norman DeJong, an ardent Calvinist who teaches education; the second is Richard John Neuhaus, a Lutheran minister and author of *The Naked Public Square*.

DeJong claims that the founding fathers did not intend "the impossible separation of church and state." Rather, congress was prohibited from "designating an *established church;* that was to remain the prerogative of the separate states."[10] He

10. DeJong, "Separation of Church and State: Historical Reality or Judicial Myth?" *Fides et Historia* 18 (Jan. 1986): 27.

claims, much in the spirit of George Goldberg in *Reconsecrating America*, that the "wall of separation was not put firmly in place until 1974."[11] It is his contention that the Supreme Court under the leadership of Justice Hugo Black grievously erred when it rendered the *Everson v. Board of Education* decision and when Black, in support of the court's decision, lifted the phrase "wall of separation" from a letter Thomas Jefferson had written to the Danbury Baptist Association. "For Jefferson," DeJong writes, "it was a campaign promise to a selected group of political supporters. For us it has now become an intellectual nightmare and a seemingly immovable plank in American jurisprudence."[12]

For DeJong, as for many others who desperately want "somebody to do something" about the moral collapse of the nation, this attempt to interpret American history in favor of the establishment of religion has a certain appeal. However, if the malaise of America is rooted in the loss of personal integrity, the breakup of the family, the failure of the public school system to either discipline or educate for a democratic society, the breakdown of law and order throughout the land, and the failure of the churches to convince their members that Christianity involves personal discipleship, how does the restructuring of society with the union of church and state address these problems?

The Naked Public Square by Richard John Neuhaus, while sympathetic to the New Right and its religious agenda, constitutes a far more subtle and sophisticated appeal for some form of religious establishment than most of the New Right propaganda. Although not in total agreement with Jerry Falwell and the Moral Majority, Neuhaus uses this New Right movement as a springboard for his critique of the American religious situation, which leaves the country with what he calls a "naked public square":

> The truly naked public square is at best a transitional phenomenon. It is a vacuum begging to be filled. When the democratically affirmed institutions that generate and transmit values are excluded, the vacuum will be filled by the agent left in control of the public square, the state. In this manner, a perverse notion of

11. Ibid.
12. Ibid.

the disestablishment of religion leads to the establishment of the state as church.[13]

Certainly a "perverse notion" of disestablishment would lead one to think that the First Amendment disenfranchised Christians, which it did not. What it did was free American society from religious warfare and the persecution of religious minorities which had cursed Europe for more than a thousand years. It also provided religious freedom with its most secure guarantee. Neuhaus recognizes the value of the concept while quarreling with Jefferson's wording when he writes,

> The "separation of church and state," as Jefferson somewhat misleadingly termed it, is essential to check the pretensions of the church. More important, and more pertinent to the constitutional intent, it is necessary to check the pretensions of the state. The "no establishment" clause, it needs ever to be repeated, is in the service of the "free exercise" clause. The primary reason for the "no establishment" clause is not to prevent the church from taking over the state but to prevent the state from taking over the church.[14]

This statement as it stands is misleading. While the First Amendment today protects the church from inordinate demands of the state, this surely was not the issue that called forth this amendment in the first place. Only an examination of the historical forces which converged in 1786 to disestablish the Protestant Episcopal Church in Virginia and which insisted upon a bill of rights incorporating guarantees of religious freedom for the new nation can explain "the original intent" of the First Amendment.

The Reconstruction Movement

This relatively small but increasingly influential movement constitutes possibly the harshest "new dissident" criticism of

13. Neuhaus, *The Naked Public Square*, p. 86.
14. Ibid., p. 116.

the First Amendment and the implied *institutional* separation of church and state. If the advocates of this radical reordering of American society have their way, religious freedom will vanish. The question naturally arises: Who are these people, and what kind of a society do they envision for the nation?

On the surface they appear to be a deeply dedicated and highly motivated group of Christians determined to implement what they consider to be biblical principles in the restructuring of American society. By the term "biblical," they mean the teachings of the Old Testament. They too are the heirs of Calvin for whom Geneva and the Puritan colonies of New England provide a pattern for implementing their concept of a Christian state. They are also fond of citing Francis Schaeffer and his more radical son, Franky, to support their views. However, according to one of the more vocal Reconstructionists—Gary North of Tyler, Texas—the elder Schaeffer failed to call for a theocracy, which, according to North, is the biblical ideal.

Thus, if they had their way, the Reconstructionists would replace democracy with theocracy. In this theocracy, "God's Law" would prevail. This law is found in the Bible, which the Reconstructionists refer to as a "military handbook." According to their application of biblical law, the death penalty would be exacted in cases of adultery, homosexuality, murder (in which they include abortion), and incorrigible children, just as it was in ancient Israel. A flat ten-percent tax would also be levied in place of the present income tax structure. In addition, "God's Law" would be applied in every area of life.

Some Reconstructionists hold that their vision of society is supported by the Westminster Confession of Faith, of which they claim to be the true heirs. Reverend Rousas John Rushdoony, apparently the major architect of the Reconstruction movement, credits Professor Cornelius Van Til of Westminster Theological Seminary for the seminal ideas that provided his chief inspiration. There is little doubt that Rushdoony, who has some thirty books to his credit, is the movement's leading thinker. But his son-in-law, Gary North, with whom he admits he has some differences, now rivals Rushdoony in influence.

North insists that a clear understanding of the Christian

faith is an essential element in the movement. It could be argued, however, that the Reconstructionists have only a partial understanding of it, since they draw their teachings largely from selected passages from the Old Testament and could exist quite independently of Christ and the New Testament. North emphasizes four "key doctrines": (1) divine predestination, (2) presuppositional apologetics, (3) optimistic eschatology, and (4) the comprehensiveness of God's law.[15] North views the conflict in which the Reconstructionists are engaged with the American system as cosmic. "The issue is sovereignty: God vs. Satan, Christianity vs. secular humanism, family vs. state."[16] The archenemy is secular humanism, which, according to North, has captured the centers of power and influence in church and state—under its sway are judges, educators, mainline church officials, and "especially seminary professors."[17]

In North's wide-ranging attack against American democracy, the public schools come in for considerably more attention than most of his targets. According to North, the public schools have taken on the function of the family, to which the education of children properly belongs. Since the public schools promote secular humanism, that has become the established religion of the country. According to David Chilton, one of North's disciples, this tragic course of events began with Horace Mann, who held that education was the responsibility of the state.[18] Some Reconstructionists hold that public schools will no longer be necessary after the movement has remade America into the New Israel, because families will then be in charge of education through their own Christian schools. In the meantime, they seek ways of securing government funds for parochial-school students in the form of vouchers, tax relief, and direct support without government controls.

15. North, "Tactics of Christian Resistance," in *Christianity and Civilization*, ed. James B. Jordan and Gary North (Tyler, Tex.: Geneva Divinity School, 1983), p. xliv.

16. Ibid., p. xix.

17. Ibid., p. xxx.

18. Gary North and David Chilton, "Apologetics and Strategy," in *Christianity and Civilization*, p. 102.

While the goals of this "utopian vision" seem to be rather farfetched, an "impossible dream," the advocates of the Reconstruction movement go on their self-assured way, reinterpreting the First Amendment as they please without either a theological or a historical understanding of its significance. Sympathetic to their view are two constitutional lawyers, John Eidsmoe, author of *God and Caesar: Christian Faith and Political Action*, and John W. Whitehead, author of *The Second American Revolution*. According to them, America was founded on Christian principles and is therefore a Christian nation. Accordingly, even if separation of church and state was intended by the First Amendment in some sense, it did not apply to the states. Eidsmoe argues, "The founders intended to prohibit two things: (1) Any attempt by the federal government to establish a national religion; and (2) any attempt by the federal government to interfere with the various state churches."[19] Only a superficial understanding of the historical process in Revolutionary America could support the second of these two assertions. Later in the book he seems to contradict himself when he says that it is not government's responsibility to promote virtue, morality, or community.[20] If America is a Christian nation, as Eidsmoe claims, then it would appear that the government is responsible for "virtue," "morality," and "community." He is surely far from the mark when he makes Jesus into a warrior-prophet in the likeness of Muhammad. This caricature of Christ is understandable only in the context of the New Right's religious and political agenda, much of which they share with the Reconstructionists.

The way in which these dissidents interpret the Constitution and the First Amendment is hardly new. More than forty years ago the pre–Vatican II American Catholic hierarchy was highly critical of the concept of separation. When the Supreme Court declared that the First Amendment intended to erect a "wall of separation between church and state," a vigorous debate

19. Eidsmoe, *God and Caesar: Christian Faith and Political Action* (Westchester, Ill.: Crossway Books, 1984), p. 20.
20. Ibid., p. 77.

broke out. The Catholic bishops adopted the interpretation of
James M. O'Neill, a Catholic author who labeled "spurious" the
"great American principle of complete separation of church and
state."[21] As Leo Pfeffer points out in *Church, State, and Freedom*, this position was assumed despite the fact that "the most
authoritative Catholic text[book] on church and state in America, published four years before the Everson decision [1947],
stated: 'Our Federal and state constitutions forbid the legal
establishment of any form of religion thereby insuring the
separation of Church and state.'"[22]

The Reconstructionists are but echoing much of this earlier
discontent with the First Amendment and its interpretation. At
the same time, they are joining the New Right in making common
cause with some traditional dissidents who prior to the American
Revolution entertained visions of an establishment of religion in
the New World. Although the chorus is mixed, they do sing the
same notes often enough to enable the audience to recognize that
the song is hardly "freedom's song."

A CONCERTED EFFORT

Admittedly the phrase "separation of church and state" lacks
precision and, therefore, must be defined. However, it has won
wide acceptance and is probably the best phrase to express the
"no establishment and free exercise" clause of the First Amendment. At least this was Jefferson's interpretation of the First
Amendment. In the famous letter he wrote on January 1, 1802,
to the Danbury Baptist Association, Jefferson said,

> Believing with you that religion is a matter which lies solely
> between man and his God, that he owes account to none other
> for his faith or his worship, that the legislative powers of govern-
> ment reach actions only, and not opinions, I contemplate with

21. Pfeffer, *Church, State, and Freedom* (Boston: Beacon Press,
1953), p. 118.
22. Ibid.

sovereign reverence that act of the whole American people which declared that their legislature should "make no law respecting an establishment of religion, or prohibiting the free exercise thereof," thus building a wall of separation between church and state. Adhering to this expression of the supreme will of the Nation in behalf of the rights of conscience, I shall see with sincere satisfaction the progress of those sentiments which tend to restore to man his natural rights, convinced he has no natural right in opposition to his social duties.[23]

The First Amendment did mean to insure the *institutional* separation of church and state. However, it did not intend to disenfranchise Christians or keep them from being the "salt, light, and leaven" of Christ's vision in any given society. There is no way this amendment can be interpreted as divorcing a public figure from his personal faith and value system. It is a "people document," designed to guarantee the religious rights of the citizens of the new nation, to protect them from religious tyranny by church or state. The colonials of the New World had experienced both. The Revolutionary War was fought to free the colonies and their citizens of one, and the First Amendment was designed to free them once and for all from the other. If this is a fairly accurate understanding of the intent of the First Amendment, then why the rising tumult against the separation of church and state, especially by those who stand to lose the most by its abandonment? In other words, what lies behind this concerted effort to discard the First Amendment?

Parochial school systems are terribly expensive to maintain, especially if they are to compete successfully with the public schools. The clamor for vouchers for students and/or tax breaks for parents or even public funds for church schools seems to indicate that the immediate motivation behind repealing the amendment is financial support. One of the surest ways to invite the government to meddle in the religious instruction of private schools is to seek and accept financial aid from the government. For what the government supports it will eventually control.

23. Jefferson, cited by Joseph Martin Dawson in *Baptists and the American Republic* (Nashville: Broadman Press, 1956), p. 127.

Some religious schools have discovered this through experience. Of course, the Reconstructionists' vision of a restructured America has made a new parochial school system a must, because this is where indoctrination would take place. And what kind of society would result from their ideology? At first an increasingly fragmented one. Eventually, if they achieved their goals, a new America would emerge not wholly unlike ancient Israel.

While the Reconstruction movement represents the New Right's extreme flanks, there are common concerns, common presuppositions, and common goals that characterize every segment of the movement. The determination to do something about the moral decadence of American society is a common response triggered by the legalization of abortion on demand. As if this were a common signal to organize and "vocalize," fundamentalists, who had previously taken little interest in national politics, seemed to become politically active overnight. They proceeded to organize numerous national political-action groups, the most prominent of which was Jerry Falwell's Moral Majority.[24] They also aligned themselves with the Republican party and in 1988 attempted to control the party in the interest of electing one of their own, Pat Robertson. They didn't succeed, but their failure will probably result only in a shift in strategy, not bring an end to their political action on behalf of their religious agenda.

During the Reagan years, the New Religious Right made significant progress in changing the character of the Supreme Court. It appears that they also enjoyed some success in enlisting the Reagan administration in "bringing America back to God and old-fashioned family values," despite some misgivings about Reagan's rapprochement with the Soviet Union and revelations regarding the president's use of astrology and good-luck charms.[25] In the process the New Right has taken a course

24. For a listing of the rash of books and major articles published on or by the New Religious Right, see Richard V. Pierard, *Bibliography on the New Christian Right* (Terre Haute, Ind.: Richard V. Pierard, 1981).

25. For a succinct exposé of the New Right role in the political process and the use of evangelicals and fundamentalists, see Richard V. Pierard, "Religion and the 1984 Election Campaign," *Review of Religious Research* 27 (Dec. 1985).

fraught with peril, even attempting to make the Republican party the vehicle of a civil religion. Charles Colson, who knows by experience the tragic consequences of the breakdown of integrity in the highest levels of government, detects danger in the New Right's religious agenda: "The conservative argument is, 'Bring America back to God and old-fashioned values.' Certainly, I am all for bringing America back to its traditional values. But I think there is a grave danger when we begin to talk that way, for it would amount to creating civil religion in the land, that is, putting the state and God on the same basis."[26]

Colson, who since his conversion has shown an exemplary personal commitment to Christ, should be heard on this point. Not only does the attempt to commandeer the state on behalf of the church confuse the roles of both state and church, but to make Christianity the religion of the state is to rob it of its universal character and to reduce the Almighty to a national icon. Then Christianity becomes little more than cheap nationalism to be manipulated in the interests of the state. The missionary witness is thereby greatly impaired, if not nullified. In the process the nation is not saved, and the church is lost.[27]

A BETTER WAY

How does one discover an alternative to the New Religious Right and those who seek to restore some form of an established church in "the naked public square"? The New Testament has not left us without direction in this regard. The guidelines are found primarily in the unique and personal revelation of God in Christ, which was historically mediated, a fact to which the New Testament bears authentic witness. With Balthasar Hub-

26. Colson, *The Role of the Church in Society* (Wheaton, Ill.: Victor Books, 1986), p. 13.
27. For a revealing article on the relationship of Southern Baptists' fundamentalist leaders with the Reconstruction movement, see Steve Fox, "Why SBC Right Upset with Dunn and Baptist Joint Committee," in *SBC Today*, Jan. 1989, p. 20.

maier and Roger Williams, I believe that religious freedom is rooted and grounded in the Incarnation. Christ came to invite men and women to salvation, not to coerce the consciences of the unwilling. Therefore, we conclude that religious freedom is not a luxury or something that can be given or withheld at the whim of the state but a God-given right. This is the conviction that fueled the struggle recorded in the following pages.

This work is one attempt to put the current debate over the role of religion in American life in its proper historical context. Obviously, it is impossible to tell the whole story of the human struggle to be free from the tyrannies that would enslave and destroy. Therefore, major attention will be given to the American struggle for religious freedom, a struggle in which dissenters played a significant role in helping to shape the character of the new nation in the process of birth two centuries ago.

Chapter II

The Continental Cradle

In 1651, John Clarke, pastor of the Newport Baptist Church in the Rhode Island colony, expressed the opinion that "New England was becoming old and Old England was becoming new." This rather pointed evaluation was based upon his own bitter experience of persecution at the hands of Massachusetts Bay authorities.

At the request of a blind man (a William Witter of Lynn, near Boston), Clarke, along with two men of his church, Obadiah Holmes and John Crandall, had been conducting a worship service when constables interrupted and hauled the three men off to jail. Holmes was publicly whipped in front of the Boston State House; Clarke was spared this fate only because a bystander paid his fine. Small wonder, then, that the Bay Colony didn't fare too well when Clarke compared Governor Endicott's Massachusetts and Cromwell's England.

Fourteen years earlier, Clarke had arrived in Boston, fleeing the persecuting fervor of Archbishop William Laud. He came with the highest expectations of a new life in a new land only to run headlong into the intolerance of the Massachusetts theocracy led by Dr. John Cotton. In attempting to assist Mrs. Anne Hutchinson and her antinomian followers in moving from Boston, Clarke made contact with Roger Williams, who assisted Clarke in purchasing land from the Indians on Aquidneck (Rhode) Island.

Subsequently Clarke and Williams worked together to establish a colony that would provide a refuge for the persecuted. Both well knew what every citizen of New England should have known: that Puritans, Separatists, Baptists, and Quakers—all Nonconformists—were historically no strangers to persecution. In New England, however, the Puritans of Boston and the Separatists of Plymouth joined forces in suppressing dissent—and Baptists and, later, Quakers were numbered among the victims.

In fact, Baptists were born amid the fires of persecution. Of the first four pastors of record, two died in exile from their native England, and two died in Newgate prison. Williams must have had these men in mind as well as a long line of martyrs when, in 1644, he formulated the first of his arguments against persecution in *The Bloudy Tenent of Persecution for Cause of Conscience:* "That the blood of so many hundred thousand soules of Protestants and Papists, spilt in the Wars of present and former Ages, for their respective Consciences, is not required nor accepted by Jesus Christ the Prince of Peace." Williams got his information about persecution from the source available to every Englishman: John Foxe's *Book of Martyrs,* which, since its first appearance in English in 1563, had provided Englishmen with a sympathetic account of Christian martyrdom from the first century through the Marian years. The first edition was 1800 pages long; a greatly enlarged two-volume edition followed in 1570. Numerous subsequent editions appeared, and through the nineteenth century hardly an English household could be found that did not possess at least one copy.[1]

Unfortunately, few Americans today are familiar with this monumental work, and most of those who are know only abridged and inferior versions. Therefore, before turning to the remarkable pilgrimage of John Smyth and his Separatist church of Gainsborough, out of which arose the first English Baptist church (an assertion which can be documented), we need to take a brief historical excursion. In the process, we will discover the birth of an idea—religious freedom—in the midst of the fires of

1. Glanmor Williams, *Reformation Views of Church History,* ed. Martin Marty et al. (London: Lutterworth Press, 1970), p. 48.

persecution. It was the Continental cradle that nurtured the concept born across the waters that was to shape the foundations of the American republic.

"THE CHURCH STOOPS TO CONQUER"

Christianity early found itself the object of severe persecution. Within the Roman empire it was an illegal religion and thus fair game for its "competitors"; most of all, it was the scapegoat of Roman emperors, beginning with Nero. After two-and-a-half centuries of intermittent persecution of varying intensity, relief came in terms of an imperial edict, the Edict of Milan, issued in 313. Two years before, shortly before his death, Emperor Galerius had issued an Edict of Toleration. Although the Edict of Milan spelled out a broader toleration than its predecessor—indeed, was the most generous document up to that point—its provisions were by no means certain until Constantine became the sole emperor and patron of the church.

As *Pontifex Maximus*, he assumed the role of the head of the church even before he was baptized. His favors on behalf of the church and its leaders were numerous. The church had indeed conquered—or so it seemed. But if Constantine had hoped to use the church to hold together his decadent empire, he was mistaken. The church was soon divided into rival factions. Constantine resorted to the sword against the Donatists to try to compel conformity, but this attempt failed. Even the Council of Nicea in 325—over which Constantine himself presided—failed to achieve unity among Catholic Christians. Banishment became the lot of the losing faction. But what was far more damaging than the defeat of Arius and his sympathizers was the pattern thus established: that of using the state to enforce the will of the church. The church did triumph in a technical sense, but it became hopelessly secularized in the process.

That which began with Constantine was theologically undergirded by Augustine and was incorporated into the empire by Theodosius I. With the formation of the Holy Roman Empire, Charlemagne carried out the policies of patronage thus established by ordering the death of every Saxon who chose to remain unbaptized.[2] The church benefited greatly from Charlemagne's patronage; with it the power and prestige of the papacy were enhanced. Consequently, the church increasingly sought to use the state for its own ends. Perhaps the clearest statement of this policy of the medieval church was the papal bull entitled *Unam Sanctam*, issued by Boniface VIII in 1302. The words were those of the curia, but the theory had been formulated by Aquinas. Thus the pope felt quite sure that both Edward I of England and Philip IV of France would bow to his dictum. Although the bull did not have its desired effect, it is representative of the most exalted claims made by the Roman Catholic Church over the governments of this world.

> We are told by the word of the gospel that in this His fold there are two swords,—a spiritual, namely, and a temporal. For when the apostles said "Behold here are two swords"—when, namely, the apostles were speaking in the church—the Lord did not reply that this was too much, but enough. Surely he who denies that the temporal sword is in the power of Peter wrongly interprets the word of the Lord when He says: "Put up thy sword in its scabbard." Both swords, the spiritual and the material, therefore, are in the power of the church; the one, indeed, to be wielded for the church, the other by the church; the one by the hand of the priest, the other by the hand of kings and knights, but at the will and sufferance of the priest. One sword, moreover, ought to be under the other, and the temporal authority to be subjected to the spiritual.[3]

The "two sword" doctrine was not new, but this was the first time it was enshrined in a papal encyclical. Upon this assumption the popes appealed to the monarchs of Europe to field their armies against Islam during the Crusades. Accord-

2. Leonard Verduin, *The Anatomy of a Hybrid: A Study in Church-State Relationships* (Grand Rapids: Wm. B. Eerdmans, 1976), p. 121.
3. *The Papal Encyclicals in Their Historical Context*, ed. Anne Fremantle (New York: New American Library, 1963), p. 73.

ingly, the Crusades more than any other single event or series of
events changed the way Christendom viewed war. Despite previous attempts at establishing the "peace of God," in the
Crusades the church embraced war as a means of meeting the
Muslim threat. Innocent III sent a crusading army against the
Albigenses and Waldenses, promising the same spiritual benefits
that he had promised to those fighting the Turks. The crusading
armies also spawned several military orders such as the Knights
Templars, the Calatravas, and the Santiagos. This development
represented the ultimate capitulation of the church to the warrior
syndrome, for these were not knights of some secular ruler
fighting on behalf of the church—they *were* the church.

Pope Innocent III also led the Fourth Lateran Council (the
most important council of the Middle Ages) to initiate a reor-
ganization of the Inquisition, which, under the supervision of
the bishops, had been somewhat ineffective. By 1262 an inquisitor general had been appointed with headquarters in Rome.
Monarchs and other secular rulers were enlisted in the fight to
suppress the growing menace of heresy. Technically, the Holy
Office, with the help of various orders (mainly the Dominicans),
was to uncover heretics by interrogation and trial. Those condemned were then committed to the civil authorities for punishment. But even this neat division between the functions of
church and state broke down in numerous cases when zealous
monks, intent upon gaining a confession or a conversion, took
a life in the process of torture.

The Spanish Inquisition under the Inquisitor General
Tomás de Torquemada reached a level of efficiency and secrecy
unequaled elsewhere. According to Llorente, onetime secretary
of the Inquisition in Spain, an estimated 114,000 victims were
accused of heresy during Torquemada's eighteen-year reign of
terror. Of these, 10,220 were burned to death, and 97,000 were
sentenced to life imprisonment or to perpetual acts of public
penance.[4]

4. In recent studies, the accuracy of Llorente's account of the
Inquisition in Spain has been called into question. For a variety of scholarly
evaluations of the nature and influence of the Spanish Inquisition, see

Of course, there are those who say, "This all happened long ago and far away. No right-thinking person would want to reactivate such a chamber of horrors out of one of Western civilization's most terrifying nightmares." Yet we must not underestimate the powers of darkness or the capacity of the human heart for self-deception. Take, for example, the opinion of Miguel de la Pinta Llorente, a modern Spanish scholar: he claims that the Inquisition saved Spain from the sins and iniquities of the secular state.[5]

THE REFORMATION ERA

The dark chapter that witnessed the executions of John Huss and Jerome of Prague and the senseless burning of Wycliffe's bones appeared destined to come to an end with the writings of Erasmus against war and Luther's insistence in 1522 that hearts be won so that consciences not be violated by coercive measures on behalf of reform. But it soon became evident that Erasmus did not mean to exempt "heretics" from the death penalty, and by 1531 Luther was on record as approving execution as a cure for Anabaptism.[6]

As Europe's state churches began to take shape, the fires of persecution were kindled afresh as Catholic states burned both Anabaptists and Protestants and as Protestant states executed both Catholics and Anabaptists. The Reformed Church under the leadership of Zwingli set the precedent when Zwingli's Zürich put to death the first Anabaptist to die at the hands of Protestants and took up the sword to promote the

---

Paul J. Hauben, *The Spanish Inquisition* (New York: John Wiley & Sons, 1969). Surprisingly enough, there are some modern defenders of this institution of repression.

5. Cited by Hauben, ibid., pp. 27-29.

6. For a detailed description of Luther's changing attitude toward the Anabaptists, see Walther Köhler, "Martin Luther," in *The Mennonite Encyclopedia*, vol. 3 (Scottdale, Pa.: Mennonite Publishing House, 1957), pp. 419-20, section G.

Reformed faith against the Catholic cantons. And before the end of the sixteenth century, other new Protestant state churches had followed suit. Simply to mention Felix Manz, Michael Sattler, Claus Felbinger, Michael Servetus, Joan of Kent, Archbishop Thomas Cranmer, and Constantino de la Fuente is to call to mind an era in which law was made to serve "the ultimate moral concerns" of the citizens of half a dozen different nations. Those who dissented from the established churches were effectively silenced—or were they?

On February 27, 1528, an earnest young Scotsman by the name of Patrick Hamilton was burned to death for his faith. The fagots were damp, and the fire burned hesitantly, prolonging his agony some six hours. During this time his courage, faith, and Christian forbearance put to shame those who sought to stifle the gospel by burning those who proclaimed it. Upon this occasion a friend of Archbishop Beaton is reported to have admonished him, "My Lord, if ye burn any more, except ye follow my counsel, ye will destroy yourselves. If ye will burn them, let them be burnt in [low] cellars; for the reik (i.e. smoke) of Maister Patrik Hammylton has infected as many as it blew upon."[7]

What was said of Patrick Hamilton's martyrdom could also be said of the entire history of religious persecution. Few deny that Mary Tudor's policy of wholesale execution of the Protestant minority, Anglican and Anabaptist, did more to advance the cause of Protestantism than Edward's five years of benevolent rule. But perhaps the vacillating policies of the English crown produced more hypocrites and skeptics than true believers of any faith. This was surely the conviction that marked the Anabaptist witness.

7. Cited by A. M. Renwick in *The Story of the Scottish Reformation* (Grand Rapids: Wm. B. Eerdmans, 1960), p. 26.

THE ANABAPTIST WITNESS

Maligned and despised by both Protestants and Catholics, the Anabaptists of the sixteenth century became the "church under the cross." Their refusal to recognize infant baptism as true baptism and the state churches of Luther and Zwingli as true churches caused both church and state to brand them as anarchists.[8] But for those who cared to know the truth, it was clear that while the Anabaptists rejected the sacral society of medieval creation, they did not reject the state but rather redefined its role according to their understanding of the church.

The Anabaptists first attempted to form a church after the New Testament pattern in the canton of Zürich in January 1525. The local church, as they envisioned it, was to be based upon a personal commitment to Christ and voluntary submission to baptism by water. This meant that only adult believers could be members. Such a concept cut across both the traditional parish church pattern and the traditional doctrine of infant baptism. By implication the Anabaptists called for a reordering of society that would greatly limit the role of government in religious affairs.

Although most Anabaptists were unlearned artisans and peasants, virtually all shared a common understanding about the necessity of the new birth *(Wiedergeburt)*, believers' baptism, the nature of discipleship *(Nachfolge Christi)*, the church *(Gemeinde)*, and the limitations of the magistrates' *(Obrigkeit)* authority. To the state belonged the sword for the purpose of maintaining law and order, and to the church alone belonged the responsibility to discipline its own members, and that by spiritual means only. The evangelistic and missionary thrust of the movement led to some variations in the implementation of the ideal and to vigorous opposition by Anabaptist opponents.

The treatment that the Anabaptists experienced at the

8. In *The Reformers and Their Stepchildren* (Grand Rapids: Wm. B. Eerdmans, 1964), Leonard Verduin points out that Luther and Zwingli experienced two phases in their attitude toward the "stepchildren," moving from ambiguity to open opposition as they came to define the church as a body that embraced "all in a given locality" (pp. 17-18).

hands of their enemies led to a variety of Anabaptist responses. While some began to talk of taking up arms to defend themselves, this idea was quickly rejected by all factions among them. The Schleitheim Confession and Balthasar Hubmaier's *On the Sword* defined two different attitudes toward the state. Hubmaier held that a Christian could be a magistrate and because of his faith a better one at that; the Schleitheim Confession took a more negative position. But both ruled out the magistrate's authority within the church. The Anabaptists also developed a theology of martyrdom which held that suffering was a mark of the true church, and that although martyrdom was not the goal of the Christian life, it was not to be shunned. In addition, the Anabaptists were the first in the sixteenth century to develop a thoroughgoing position on religious liberty based upon their understanding of the nature of faith, the gospel, and the church.

The Anabaptists were convinced that God had spoken his last word in Jesus Christ. This conviction also distinguished their call for religious freedom both from previous pleas (those of Marsilius of Padua and Erasmus, for example) and from subsequent positions of rationalists and Deists operating upon agnostic assumptions of the French Enlightenment. In short, this Anabaptist conviction had a basis both biblical and theological, with profound implications for the understanding of the nature of the church and its relation to the state.

BALTHASAR HUBMAIER

Balthasar Hubmaier, onetime cathedral preacher at Regensburg and John Eck's colleague on the faculty of the University of Ingolstadt, articulated most clearly the Anabaptist position on religious freedom in a tract entitled *Concerning Heretics and Those Who Burn Them (Von Ketzern und ihren Verbrennern)*. Having been driven from his church and Waldshut by the threat of Austrian intervention, Hubmaier sought refuge in the Swiss city of Schaffhausen. Here the Benedictine monastery was in a state of dissolution, and thus provided a perfect shelter for the fugitive. Even though the traditional right of sanctuary should have given Hubmaier some sense of security, Austria was pressuring Schaffhausen to turn the renegade priest over to the authorities. Waldshut, where Hubmaier's church was located, was under Austrian jurisdiction. Therefore, he addressed three petitions to the City Council of Schaffhausen, asking to be heard while at the same time denying the authority of the magistrates in religious affairs. Accordingly, he also made this assertion:

> Paul also calls the [secular] power servants of God *[Dienerin]*. The judge then is God's servant so here on earth in God's place he shall sit and govern. But in matters pertaining to a man's relationship with God, God has spoken in these matters one should not be afraid but declare with Moses that judgment is God's and say with the holy apostles, who were also forbidden by the magistrate that they henceforth no more should speak in the name of Jesus; "Man must obey God more than men."[9]

Hubmaier went on to instruct the council about the balance between truth and judgment. He asserted, "We still have clearer light in Christ than in Moses and the Prophets. Thereby he will give us the meaning of the Scriptures as he further says: 'Search the Scriptures for they were given as a witness to me.'"[10] Repeatedly Hubmaier appealed to Scripture as the highest criterion by which he and his work must be judged. If a man attempts to sit in judgment over God's Word, Hubmaier claimed, he is a false prophet, for no man can sit in judgment over God's Word. Such a person is like Lucifer, who wished to make himself into a god—such a man sits in judgment over God. This, for Hubmaier, was the ultimate blasphemy.

Even though Hubmaier did not succeed in securing the public hearing that he desired, he was allowed to remain in the

---

9. *Balthasar Hubmaier Schriften*, ed. Gunnar Westin and Torsten Bergsten (Heidelberg: Verein für Reformationsgeschichte, 1962), p. 82, author's translation. For a more complete discussion of the situation and the petitions, see William R. Estep, *Anabaptist Beginnings (1523-1533)* (Nieuwkoop: B. de Graaf, 1976), pp. 43, 46.

10. Ibid.

monastery for about two months. While there, he wrote *Concerning Heretics*. This work is an abstract of principles on religious liberty that Hubmaier derived from the nature of the gospel, the church, and the state. These are possibly the most revolutionary set of ideas about the subject that the sixteenth century produced. While many of the same concepts that surfaced in the petitions *(Eerbietungen)* are also found in this work, the petitions were personal appeals of an obviously distressed priest. *Concerning Heretics*, on the other hand, was a closely reasoned treatise arguing not merely for toleration but for complete religious freedom as a universal principle.[11]

At the outset, Hubmaier challenged the medieval definition of heresy and heretics. Regardless of how one defines them, he asserted, heretics are not to be intimidated by force: "But a Turk or a heretic will not be won by our act, neither with sword nor fire but alone with patience and prayer, so we with long suffering, await the judgment of God."[12] According to Hubmaier, the only weapon the Christian has in the warfare with heresy is the Sword of the Spirit, the Word of God.

Once condemned by ecclesiastical authorities, the heretic was, according to medieval practice, "turned over to secular authority for punishment." Hubmaier denounced the whole procedure. To the sin of murder, the church had added duplicity, a crime in which the state had become involved. While recognizing the right of the state to punish criminals, even to execute them, Hubmaier denied the state that right in religious matters. Even in the case of an atheist, Hubmaier argued, the magistracy has no authority to coerce, intimidate, or punish for a lack of faith in God. In article twenty-two, he stated this radical concept very clearly: "Therefore, it is well and good that the secular authorities put to death the criminals who do physical harm to the defenseless, Romans 13. But the atheist *[gotssfind]* may no

11. Torsten Bergsten disagrees with this assessment. In *Balthasar Hubmaier*, trans. Irwin J. Barnes and William R. Estep (Valley Forge, Pa.: Judson Press, 1978), Bergsten argues that *Concerning Heretics* was not meant for universal application (pp. 131-32). I believe that just the opposite is the case.

12. *Balthasar Hubmaier Schriften*, p. 98, author's translation.

one injure, who wants for himself nothing other than to forsake the gospel."[13] Similarly, in the twenty-fourth article of his treatise Hubmaier underlined the limitations of the magistrate's power: "The [secular] authority *[gwalt]* judges criminals but not the ungodly, who may not injure body or soul, but are much more needy so that God can wisely draw good out of evil."[14]

These articles express one of Hubmaier's basic principles. He believed that the matter of one's faith, its nature or its total absence, is of no concern to the state. By promoting this belief, Hubmaier was advocating not anarchy but religious liberty. Thus he became a political theoretician for religious reasons, basing his understanding upon the teachings of Christ (found in Matthew 13) and Romans 13.

The final section of the tract is concerned with the death penalty for heresy. Such a practice, Hubmaier asserted, does not make Christians but hypocrites. While it appears to be an act of Christian piety, in reality it is a denial of the Incarnation.[15] This is perhaps Hubmaier's most profound insight. Here he was on solid theological and biblical ground. The execution of heretics is a futile act, he went on to claim, since truth can be neither destroyed nor advanced by such an act. Hubmaier's parting shot is found in article thirty-six, in which he declared demonic the law that demanded the burning of heretics.[16] He concluded the tract with his life's motto: "truth is immortal" *(Die Warheit ist untödtlich)*.

On March 10, 1528, less than three and a half years after the appearance of *Concerning Heretics*, Hubmaier himself was burned to death for heresy in Vienna. His faithful wife, Elizabeth Hugline, was drowned three days later. Thus Hubmaier's witness was sealed by a martyr's death, graphically illustrating his life's motto.

Although most Anabaptists did not share Hubmaier's positive view of the state, his teachings on anthropology, sote-

13. Ibid., p. 99, author's translation.
14. Ibid.
15. Ibid.
16. Ibid., p. 100.

riology, baptism, and religious freedom became pervasive in Anabaptist life and thought. Claus Felbinger, who was beheaded for his faith, and Jacob Hutter, who was burned at the stake, were only two of thousands who held consistently to the principle that God wants no unwilling disciple. Sebastian Franck, Kaspar Schwenckfeld, and Sebastian Castellio championed the cause of freedom beyond Anabaptist circles.

THE MENNONITES

It was through contact with Dutch Anabaptism that bore the name of its most effective spokesman, Menno Simons, that the English Separatist John Smyth and his followers were introduced to Anabaptist teachings on religious liberty, an introduction that was to have lasting significance.

Menno Simons left the priesthood of the Roman Catholic Church at Witmarsum early in 1536. For about nine months he had wrestled with his newfound faith, trying desperately to retain his position in spite of increasing reservations. Finally, he could delay his departure no longer. Almost immediately thereafter he became the recognized champion of the Anabaptist cause, preaching valiantly against the Münsterites, who had mistakenly attempted to set up a theocratic kingdom at Münster, Germany. Very soon a price was placed on his head, and Menno became the object of a manhunt by the authorities. Consequently, he was to learn firsthand the meaning of persecution.

Written on the run, Menno's early works—*The Blasphemy of John of Leiden, The New Birth, Foundation of Christian Doctrine,* and *Christian Baptism*—contain all the familiar themes found in the writings of the Swiss and South German Anabaptists. In addition, Menno frequently went out of his way to condemn the sins of the Münsterites and to draw clear lines of distinction between the Münsterite faith and true Anabaptism, which called for suffering under the cross and a discipleship of Christ manifested in love and obedience.

Menno closed many of his works with an appeal for religious freedom.

Even though Menno chose 1 Corinthians 3:11 as his life's motto ("For no other foundation can any one lay than that which is laid, which is Jesus Christ"), he concluded his book on Christian baptism with words reminiscent of Hubmaier's motto: "Truth will remain forever unconquered, no matter how violently many fight against her."[17]

Menno died twenty-five years after becoming an Anabaptist. Half a century later his teachings were commanding a following not only among the Dutch but also among English refugees in the Netherlands. Among these were John Smyth and Thomas Helwys. John Smyth and his congregation provide the most discernible link between the Anabaptists of the Continent and the English Baptist movement.

THE EMERGENCE OF ENGLISH BAPTISTS

It appears that English Baptists first arose out of English Separatism under the influence of Continental Anabaptism. Specifically, John Smyth is the pivotal figure in this scenario. It was he who was responsible for the infusion of Anabaptist concepts into Baptist life at its very inception. The transformation of Smyth from a staunch Puritan who supported the state's right to enforce religious conformity upon all dissenters into an advocate of religious freedom was a remarkable development with few parallels in the history of the church. Accordingly, for a more complete understanding of this aspect of the development of the concept of religious freedom, we need to trace Smyth's pilgrimage in some detail.

17. *The Complete Writings of Menno Simons, c. 1496-1561*, ed. John C. Wenger (Scottdale, Pa.: Herald Press, 1956), p. 287.

John Smyth—Baptist or Mennonite?

On a wall in the entrance to the Single Canal Mennonite Church in Amsterdam there is a chart with a list of elders of the church from its inception to the present. John Smyth's name stands at the head of the list of English-speaking elders of the English congregation, which did not become an integral part of the Waterlander Church until two years after his death in 1612. In a newer section of the city there is another church that bears his name: the John Smyth Memorial Baptist Church. In other words, while Smyth has been revered for the better part of four centuries as a founding father of the English Baptist movement, he has also been honored as an elder of the Waterlander Mennonite Church.[18] Those who know little or nothing about Smyth and his spiritual pilgrimage naturally wonder how this could be. The answer lies in the remarkable changes that occurred in Smyth's life during a ten-year period, from 1602 to 1612.

John Smyth, Puritan, 1586-1605

Little is known about Smyth's early life. Apparently a bright but impoverished student, he matriculated at Christ's College, Cambridge University, in March 1586. Francis Johnson, at the time an outspoken Puritan, was his tutor. Smyth graduated with a B.A. degree in 1590. This was the same year that Johnson was expelled from the university for advocating the Presbyterian system of church government as more scriptural than the Episcopal system. With the danger of the Spanish Armada past, Queen Elizabeth turned her attention to enforcing the religious settlement of 1559 upon all her subjects. Puritans were suppressed, and three of the most articulate of the Separatist leaders—John Greenwood, Henry Barrowe, and John Penry— were executed in 1593. Although many Separatists were still in prison, hundreds began to leave London for the Netherlands. Their pastor, Francis Johnson, was released from prison in 1597

---

18. A. C. Underwood, *A History of the English Baptists* (London: Carey Kingsgate Press Limited, 1947), p. 33.

and joined his congregation in Amsterdam, which had become known as the Ancient Church.

After obtaining his B.A. degree, Smyth remained at Cambridge to work on his M.A. degree, which he received in 1593. In the Michaelmas term of 1594 he was made a fellow of Christ's College, which required him to take an oath of allegiance to church and crown. Ordination was expected to follow within the year; hence Smyth was ordained to the priesthood of the Church of England by Bishop Wickham of Lincoln. He taught at Christ's College for four years, a tenure that came to an end with his marriage, since tutors could not be married. In 1600 he became the city lecturer of Lincoln, a position he held for little more than two years.

While at Lincoln, in opposition to the Roman Catholic presence (which was still strong, according to the diocesan records), Smyth was a staunch supporter of the Anglican establishment even though he still considered himself a Puritan. His sympathies with the Puritan party were made public as early as 1592. His Lincoln years were marked by his attempt to reconcile the Calvinistic concept of the fourfold ministry with the concept of ministry held by the Church of England. In his work entitled *A Patterne of True Prayer*, published in 1605, he listed "officers of the Kingdom" as doctors (teachers), pastors, (ruling) elders, and deacons. He indicated that he was not willing to debate differences between various parties in the Reformed tradition regarding the actual function of these officers, but he went on to pay homage to the authority of the king and bishops:

> We acknowledge every King in his Kingdome, the supreme Governor in all causes and over all persons, as well ecclesiasticall, as civill, next and immediately under Christ: which prince hath authoritie to substitute ecclesiastical Magistrates according to the word, for the polity of the Church, in the exercising of jurisdiction, visitation of Churches, and ordination of Ministers; which persons in England are called Bishops.[19]

19. *The Works of John Smyth, Fellow of Christ's College, 1594-1598*, 2 vols., ed. W. T. Whitley (Cambridge: Cambridge University Press, 1915), 1:158-59.

This quotation indicates that in spite of and perhaps because of the Hampton Court Conference of 1604, in which King James had rejected the Puritan program of reform, Smyth went on record in support of the Episcopal establishment. Due to a town squabble in November 1602, he had lost his position as city lecturer even after having been re-elected for a life term only six weeks before. In 1603 he had still referred to himself as "Preacher of the Citie." If he expected *A Patterne of True Prayer* to regain him his lost position, he was disappointed. The vacancy was filled by another, and Smyth moved to Gainsborough, about eighteen miles from Lincoln, where he apparently supported himself by practicing medicine.

John Smyth, Separatist, 1606-1608

Although it is difficult to pin down Smyth's whereabouts from 1603 to 1606, he must have been settling down in Gainsborough during that time. However, he did not secure a license to serve a parish church. Apparently he led worship in the local church when the parish priest was absent. An Episcopal visitation uncovered this irregularity, and Smyth was severely reprimanded. The difficulties he had experienced at Lincoln returned to haunt him upon this occasion. Even though documentation is lacking regarding the frequency with which Smyth led divine services, the following that he soon developed would seem to indicate that it was something he did fairly often. By 1606, after nine months of deliberation and prayer with both ministers and laymen, Smyth made the fateful decision to break with the Church of England. He then led in the formation of a Separatist church. This step was only the first of several steps that led the former Cambridge scholar ever further from the Church of England.

Smyth's transformation was certainly remarkable. As late as 1605, in *A Patterne of True Prayer*, he had written, "When there is a Toleration of many Religions, . . . the kingdom of God is shouldered out a doores by the devils kingdome."[20] Smyth

20. Ibid., 1:166.

went on to insist that magistrates should be Christians and careful to enforce the laws against heretics: "wherefore the Magistrates should cause all men to worship the true God, or else punish them with imprisonment, confiscation of goods, or death as the qualitie of the cause requireth."[21] (This position was to come under careful scrutiny once Smyth and his congregation had arrived in the Netherlands.)

But by 1606, Smyth had very different ideas and convictions. According to William Bradford, one of Smyth's followers who later became the governor of Plymouth colony, Smyth drew up a brief covenant patterned after that of the Old Testament saints, one very different from the "Patterne" he had so recently embraced: "They shooke of this yoake of antichristian bondage, and as ye Lords free people, joyned them selves (by covenant of the Lord) into a church estate, in ye fellowship of ye gospell, to walke in all his waye, made known, or to be made known unto them, according to their best endeavors, whatsoever it should cost them, the Lord assisting them."[22]

For some time now in England, Separatist churches had been formed along similar lines. The covenant of Francis Johnson's church, originally in London and now in Amsterdam, was but the most recent example. However, a comparison of the two kinds of covenants reveals a remarkable difference between them. In Smyth's covenant we see—in addition to the expressed desire to walk in all the "wayes of the Lord"—both a tacit admission that those signing the covenant do not possess ultimate truth and a willingness to remain open to the Spirit's further leading. These covenanters, therefore, were not only breaking with tradition as it had found expression in the Anglican Church (which now appeared beyond the hope of reform), but were also taking a giant step—a step of faith—into an unknown future, their sole assurance being that the Lord would in time make his ways known more fully.

Separatism in England was not new. There were Separatist conventicles as early as the Elizabethan settlement, if not

21. Ibid.
22. Ibid.

earlier, though their nature is not entirely clear. As Irvin Horst has shown, there is no question that Anabaptists were in England by 1534. Although their numbers may never have been large, their influence and the fear of their influence made a significant impact upon the English religious scene. Some prominent Englishmen—among them John Bocher, Henry Hart, Robert Cooche, and Humphrey Middleton—were known to have embraced certain Anabaptist teachings.[23] However, even though there probably were Anabaptist conventicles in England, the later Separatist congregations were apparently influenced more by Calvinism imported from Geneva.

It is quite evident that by the time the Smyth-led Puritans became Separatists, Separatism in England was Calvinistic, not Anabaptist. Like Smyth, Separatists were former Puritans who refused to accept the new canons resulting from the Hampton Court Conference of 1604. They considered the Church of England beyond the hope of reform and therefore a false church, a Babylon from which they could not but separate.

Apparently the new Separatist congregation met from time to time in a number of different locations, among them the town hall in Gainsborough and the Scrooby manor house. Although, as James Coggins has shown, these Separatists counted among their number several ordained Anglican clergymen and a few members of the gentry, most were commoners. However, they were unusually well educated: 98 percent could read and write, which was considerably above both English and Dutch literacy standards of the time.[24] Given this characteristic, coupled with the fact that these were people of deep convictions and considerable influence, it is not surprising that the authorities perceived them as a threat and determined to crush this fresh outcropping of Separatism with a new wave of persecution.

Since it was reported that freedom of religion—even for English Separatists—was possible in the Netherlands, Smyth's

23. See Irvin B. Horst, *The Radical Brethren: Anabaptism and the English Reformation to 1558* (Nieuwkoop: B. de Graaf, 1972).

24. See James Robert Coggins, "John Smyth's Congregation: English Separatism, Dutch Mennonites and the Elect Nation," Ph.D. diss., University of Waterloo, 1986, pp. 41-44.

entire church, which by 1607 may have numbered 150 or more, decided to leave England for Amsterdam. William Bradford commented on the decision:

> Yet seeing them selves thus molested, and that ther was no hope of their continuance ther, by joynt consente they resolved to goe into the Low Countries, wher they heard was freedome of Religion for all men; as also how sundrie from London, & other parts of the land, had been exiled and persecuted for the same cause, & were gone thither, and lived at Amsterdam, & in other places of the land.[25]

About a year after the formation of Smyth's Separatist congregation, the members began to leave England. This pilgrimage was not without peril. Families were divided, and some of those remaining were imprisoned. A furious storm in the North Sea threatened to sink one of the boats. Finally, by the spring of 1608, the entire body had succeeded in getting to Amsterdam. Their faith had been sorely tried and their understanding of the covenant severely tested.

And the trying times continued. Smyth and a large part of the church had arrived in Amsterdam as early as the summer or fall of 1607. John Robinson, who served as pastor of the Scrooby congregation, had been among the last to arrive in 1608. By that time he discovered that Smyth was raising serious questions about the order of ministry in Francis Johnson's church and the liturgy with its dependence upon books. He also discovered that all was not well within the Ancient Church led by Johnson and Henry Ainsworth. Consequently, Robinson and William Brewster, in whose house the Scrooby branch of the Gainsborough church met with Robinson as pastor, made plans to move on to Leyden, where they settled within the year. (The church they established there became the mother church of the Pilgrim fathers of Mayflower and Plymouth fame. In Leyden Brewster became a printer and later brought to Plymouth colony the Puritan classics.) Smyth and the remaining Separatists from

25. Bradford, *Of Plymouth Plantation*, ed. Harvey Wish (New York: Capricorn Books, 1962), p. 28.

the Gainsborough area found themselves increasingly isolated from their fellow Englishmen.

Smyth and Anabaptism

Although the covenant subscribed to by Smyth and his fellow Separatists was open-ended, it apparently precluded the possibility of adopting Anabaptist concepts. In fact, Smyth regarded as dangerous the exposure to Anabaptism that his followers now faced in Amsterdam. Upon arriving in the Netherlands, he is reported to have said, "Truely wee being Now Come into a place of libertie are in Great danger if wee look not well to our wayes, for wee are like men sett upon the Iyce and therefore may ezely slyde and fall."[26] Doubtless Smyth was aware that this was precisely what had happened to some English Separatists who had come from London with the Ancient Church before it settled in Amsterdam. Some had returned to England before the turn of the century full of stories about their experiences at Kampen and Naarden in 1594. Nevertheless, Smyth was a man of integrity and courage. He remained open to the truth as he understood it, regardless of its source—and over time he began to see Anabaptism as a source of truth.

Once the New Testament had become Smyth's *regla fidei*, his rejection of tradition became even more radical and his spiritualism more refined. Like the early Anabaptists, he and his little company were faced with achieving a scriptural balance between tradition and Spirit. And Smyth, like those Anabaptists, was severely criticized: even before he adopted believer's baptism, his radical rejection of tradition made him the target of misunderstanding and ridicule. On two points—involving the nature of the ministry of each particular church and its worship—he questioned both the Anglicans and the Separatists. Fortunately, the modern student can follow Smyth's spiritual and theological pilgrimage through his numerous works, which

26. Smyth, cited by Keith L. Sprunger in *Dutch Puritanism*, vol. 31 of Studies in the History of Christian Thought (Atlantic Highlands, N.J.: Humanities Press, 1982), p. 81.

document his changing convictions. Unfortunately, however, some of these are not so precisely dated as one might wish.

In 1607, Smyth brought out his *Principles and Inferences Concerning the Visible Church*. This work was probably printed in Amsterdam. It clearly indicates that Smyth had already made a basic shift in his biblical hermeneutics. The Puritan and Calvinistic orientation, with its heavy emphasis upon the Old Testament, was replaced by an appeal to the New Testament, which alone, he argued, provided the guidelines for "administring the covenant since the death of Christ." He continued, "In this little treatise the ordinances of Christ for the dispensing of the covenant since his death are described."[27] Indeed, the work abounds in citations from the New Testament, and has only a scattering of Old Testament references. In a sense this work constituted a personal confession of faith and an apology for separating from the Church of England. It also provided the basis for Smyth's critique of contemporary churches. As such, it is foundational, the first of three works which need to be examined together to see the direction in which his thought was rapidly moving.

Smyth's *Principles and Inferences* was soon followed by *The Differences of the Churches of the Separation*. In the introduction Smyth indicated that this work was based upon the principles set forth in his previous work. This treatise indicates an intimate knowledge of the Ancient Church in Amsterdam and constitutes a thorough critique of its ministry and worship and, by inference, that of the Reformed Church and the Church of England as well. In this work one of Smyth's major concerns was the nature of true spiritual worship: "Wee hould that the worship of the new testament properly so called is spirituall proceeding originally from the hart: & that reading out of a booke (though a lawful ecclesiasticall action) is no part of spirituall worship, but rather the invention of the man of synne it beeing substituted for a part of spirituall worship."[28]

Up to this point Smyth's position represented the most radical critique of his fellow Separatists yet launched. In a sense

27. *The Works of John Smyth*, 1:250.
28. Ibid., 1:273.

it was a reaction to worship in the Anglican Church, which all Separatists considered "book-bound" and lifeless. But Smyth went beyond that, arguing that all the objections which the Separatists brought against "the reading of homilies & prayers may be applyed agaynst the reading of translations in tyme of worship."[29] His major objection seems to have been based upon the nature of all translations of the Bible, which he held to be commentaries; thus, using them in worship fell into the category of reading prayers or singing Psalms. He apparently believed in serious and thorough Bible study, undertaken in the biblical languages if possible. He did not object to the reading of Scripture prior to preaching or actually engaging in worship, but he drew the line between liturgical reading and true spiritual worship, which comes from the heart. In worship the Spirit must have full sway. Smyth cited many passages of Scripture and numerous examples from both the Old and the New Testament to support his position. Above all he appealed to the example of Christ.

By discouraging the use of books in worship, Smyth apparently hoped to magnify the Holy Spirit's presence and leadership in the life of the church. But Smyth's opposition to the use of the English Bible in liturgy may have hardened because of the Genevan version being used in the Ancient Church and in the English Reformed Church in Amsterdam. The Geneva Bible contained notes advocating Calvinistic theology and ecclesiology, which Smyth was no longer willing to accept uncritically. That Smyth did not mean to leave Bible reading out of the activities of the church, even on a Sunday set aside for worship, is evident from a letter that Hughe and Anne Bromheade wrote to Sir William Hammerton in the fall of 1608, indicating that after a prayer was offered and one or two Bible chapters were read and exposited, the Bible was then put aside and various members of the church preached.[30]

Smyth's second major concern in *The Differences of the Churches of the Separation* was the ministry of the Ancient

29. Ibid., 1:292.
30. Champlin Burrage, *The Early English Dissenters in the Light of Recent Research (1550-1641)*, 2 vols. (1912; repr. New York: Russell & Russell, 1967), 1:236.

Church. Smyth believed that the elders of the church were to be chosen by the people. And even when thus chosen, they did not hold exclusively the privileges of preaching, teaching, praying, and singing; those privileges, Smyth asserted, belonged to all believers. The implication of this viewpoint was that Francis Johnson and Henry Ainsworth had appropriated authority to themselves which Smyth was unwilling to concede.

By 1609, Smyth and his followers had concluded that their church, which was founded upon a mutual covenant, must be disbanded and reorganized upon the basis of individual confessions of faith and believer's baptism. Smyth wrote *The Character of the Beast or The False Constitution of the Church* to provide the reasons for this action and to answer the criticisms of Richard Clifton. Clifton, a former member of Smyth's church, had left that congregation for the Ancient Church. Consequently, Smyth considered Clifton the spokesman for the English Separatists of Amsterdam and the one among them he knew best. Unfortunately, Smyth's manner of inaugurating believer's baptism by first baptizing himself became so magnified in the controversy that many Separatists seem to have lost sight of the overall significance of the event.

Nine years later, John Robinson called attention to Smyth's self-baptism:

> Mr Smith, Mr Helw:[ys] & the rest haveing vtterly dissolved, & disclaymed their former Ch:[urch] state, & ministery, came together to erect a new Ch:[urch] by baptism: vnto which they also ascribed so great virtue, as that they would not so much as pray together, before they had it. And after some streyning of courtesy, who should begin, . . . Mr Smith baptized first himself, & next Mr Helwis, & so the rest, making their particular confessions.[31]

There is an obvious answer to the question about why Smyth baptized himself—that he apparently saw no need to seek baptism at the hands of the Mennonites or from some of the English who had previously received believer's baptism in the

31. Robinson, cited in Burrage, 1:237.

Netherlands. Smyth well knew, as apparently his English critics did not, that there was historical precedent for self-baptism.

While *The Character of the Beast* suggests Anabaptist influence at a number of points, Smyth indicated that he was not yet fully convinced that the Mennonite position on the magistracy was biblical (although he was almost persuaded on this point). He also had reservations regarding the Mennonite teaching on the Incarnation, which was derived from Kaspar Schwenckfeld via Melchior Hofmann.[32]

Despite these two reservations, Smyth made it clear that he considered Mennonite churches true churches and all churches which practiced infant baptism false churches. It is equally evident that he wrote with deep conviction supported by his own careful study of the relevant New Testament passages. Despite his previous warnings about the Anabaptists, he had by all appearances become one.

The sequence of events with their accompanying changes had been rapid. In 1602 Smyth had been a staunch Puritan and Anglican; by 1606—after considerable thought, consultation, and prayer—he had become a Separatist. Upon arriving in Amsterdam in 1607, he expressed his dissatisfaction with the Separatist worship and ministry. Less than a year later, he reorganized his church on the basis of personal confessions of faith and believer's baptism. This almost certainly occurred in the fall or winter of 1608.

The rapid shifts Smyth made in his position subjected him to merciless criticism from his fellow Englishmen. His defense of his actions constitutes a classic apologetic for changing one's religious opinions.[33] With evident conviction Smyth wrote,

> The true constitution of the Chu.[rch] is of a new creature baptized into the Father, the Sonne, & the holy Ghost: The false constitution is of infants baptized: we professe therfor that al those Churches that baptise infants are of the same false constitution: & al those Chu.[rches] that baptize the new creature,

32. *The Works of John Smyth*, 2:572.
33. Ibid., 2:564.

those that are made Disciples by teaching, men confessing their faith & their sinnes, are of one true constitution.[34]

The criticism to which Smyth was subjected for his opinions began to have its effect—but probably not the one that his critics had hoped for. For one thing, Smyth was not a man easily moved by an opponent's arguments, and there were few English Separatists who argued as effectively as he did. Then, too, Smyth was never interested in debating for the sake of debate or for the satisfaction of vanquishing an opponent. His concern was for the truth as it related to Christ and his church. For another thing, Smyth became terminally ill with tuberculosis, and in the isolation caused by both his opinions and his illness, he increasingly turned to the Mennonites for fellowship. There seems little doubt that Mennonite influence played a role in Smyth's rethinking of the biblical teachings on baptism and the church.

The Character of the Beast reveals a mind in transition. In a period of time certainly no longer than a year, after reforming his church on the basis of personal confession of faith and believer's baptism, Smyth requested that his church be allowed to join the Mennonites as a true church of Christ. The letter contained the signatures of fifteen men and seventeen women, who were described as follows: "The names of the English who acknowledge this their error and repent of it, viz., that they took in hand to baptize themselves contrary to the order established by Christ, and who now wish to come to the true church of Christ as quickly as possible."[35]

The petition was also accompanied by a brief confession of faith containing twenty articles. There was very little in the twenty articles with which the Mennonites could find fault. It was also clear that the Smyth-led Separatists had abandoned their former Calvinistic soteriology. Hans de Ries, a well-educated and leading Waterlander Mennonite elder from Alkmaar who, like Smyth, practiced medicine, was anxious to accommodate the English. However, since the confession was incomplete

34. Ibid., 2:565.
35. Ibid., 2:681.

at a number of points and not explicit on others, de Ries and Lubbert Gerritsz drew up a confession of thirty-eight articles that became the basis for further negotiations. Although these negotiations never reached a satisfactory conclusion during Smyth's lifetime, the exchange of confessions stimulated both Smyth and Helwys to formulate and submit for Mennonite scrutiny new and much more carefully composed confessions on behalf of their respective congregations. Smyth's confession, which he drew up shortly before he died, numbered 100 articles in English and 102 in Dutch. This confession reveals that Smyth was one with the Mennonites even on those points that still presented problems for him when he published *The Character of the Beast.*

Smyth had begun to seek union with the Mennonites in February 1610. By this time, Helwys, his leading layman and chief supporter (along with nine or ten others), had broken with Smyth and the majority. In the following year Helwys and his followers published their own confession of faith, which William L. Lumpkin says "is rightly judged the First English Baptist Confession of Faith."[36] The major point of difference between Smyth's confession and Helwys' confession is seen in the articles on the magistracy. Consequently, *Smyth's confession of 1612 became the first confession of faith in English to set forth the principles of complete religious liberty and the separation of church and state.*

Articles 84 and 85 from the English edition of Smyth's confession are most significant for the Baptist development of the principle of religious liberty:

> 84. That the magistrate is not by virtue of his office to meddle with religion, or matters of conscience, to force or compel men to this or that form of religion, or doctrine: but to leave Christian religion free, to every man's conscience, and to handle only civil transgressions (Rom. XIII), injuries and wrongs of man against man, in murder, adultery, theft, etc., for Christ only is the king, and lawgiver of the church and conscience (James IV.12).

36. Lumpkin, *Baptist Confessions of Faith* (Philadelphia: Judson Press, 1959), p. 114.

85. That if the magistrate will follow Christ, and be His disciple, he must deny himself, take up his cross, and follow Christ; he must love his enemies and not kill them, he must pray for them, and not punish them, he must suffer persecution and affliction with Christ, and be slandered, reviled, blasphemed, scourged, buffeted, spit upon, imprisoned and killed with Christ; and that by the authority of magistrates, which things he cannot possibly do, and retain the revenge of the sword.[37]

Although it is debatable whether Smyth's document should be called a Baptist or a Mennonite confession, in a sense it is both. It is a Baptist confession in the sense that, from the time it first appeared to the present, virtually every Baptist confession has incorporated certain features derived from this confession. But in other ways it is inaccurate to call Smyth's confession Baptist. The explanation begins with article 85, where Smyth takes the position that a magistrate could not be a Christian without giving up his magistracy, and also implies the principle of nonresistance. Although this position was also held by some early English Baptists, Helwys disagreed with it. Accordingly, Helwys altered this position in his confession, and subsequently Baptists followed Helwys rather than Smyth. In "A Declaration of Faith of English People Remaining at Amsterdam in Holland," issued in 1611, Helwys and his small congregation declared in Article 24 their major point of departure from Smyth's church:

> That magistracie is a Holie ordinance off God, that every soule ought to bee in subject to it not for feare onelie but for conscience sake. . . . And therefore they may bee members off the Church of CHRIST, reteining their magistracie, for no Holie ordinance off GOD debarreth anie from being a member off CHRISTS Church.[38]

Helwys had already determined to return to England to bear witness to the truth of Christ and his church as he now understood it.[39] Accordingly, to reject the "magistracie" was unthinkable to him.

37. Ibid., p. 140.
38. Ibid., pp. 122-23.
39. Ibid., p. 115.

THE LEGACY

The day before Smyth died, he treated a patient suffering from pneumonia. The weather was bad, and since the man had no coat, Smyth gave him his own topcoat. However kind this gesture, Smyth left a far greater legacy than a coat: he left a legacy of freedom. Few in the history of the church have so single-mindedly rejected tradition at the prompting of the Spirit. Yet Smyth only articulated in English that which had been born and nurtured on the Continent. In rejecting the magistrate's role in the life of the church, Smyth was simply echoing Balthasar Hubmaier, Kaspar Schwenckfeld, Sebastian Castellio, and Menno Simons.

Chapter III

The English Connection

Although the concept of religious freedom was as impossible as it was unpalatable to the Magisterial Reformers, it sprang to life in the very fires stoked by Catholic and Protestant intolerance. Once armed with the New Testament in their own tongue, the Anabaptists developed a new concept of the church, one that forced a break with the medieval pattern of parish churches as well as the newly established state churches. What the Anabaptists suffered as a consequence was, at worst, unbridled persecution until death and, at best, exile or an uneasy truce. The protests against these consequences mounted, based not only upon the bitter experience of torture and death at the hands of those who thought they were doing God a service but also upon theological reflection. Nowhere was this fact more evident than in the writings and confessions of the English Baptists. If the seed was sown by the Anabaptists of the sixteenth century, the English Baptists of the seventeenth century were the first to cultivate it.

Those who blazed the trail among the English Baptists were an unlikely lot for such a challenge. For they conceived of nothing less than the remaking of society, yet most of them did not have the credentials one would think necessary for the task. Only a few among them were university educated; the others were artisans of various kinds. There were no John Miltons or

John Lockes among them; individuals of that stature would come later. As we have seen, John Smyth, an able theologian and earnest pastor, heads the list. Thomas Helwys, Smyth's most stalwart supporter, led a small though not insignificant group of ten to introduce into England the concepts of religious freedom and the separation of church and state, in payment for which he suffered a martyr's death. Mark Leonard Busher wrote the most thorough early treatment of the subject. John Murton, Helwys' successor, also gave his life for the cause, but not before adding some significant treatises of his own. Samuel Richardson, a wealthy London merchant, signed the First London Confession of the Particular Baptists (1644) and argued forcefully for religious freedom, borrowing freely from General Baptist sources (1610-1612). (The General Baptists arose out of the Smyth-Helwys church and held that Christ died for all and that therefore salvation was for all who believe. The Particular Baptists held that Christ died only for the elect.) These were several individuals among the shapers of the English Baptist faith who provided the indispensable link between Smyth and the architects of religious freedom in the New World.

THOMAS HELWYS AND
THE MISTERY OF INIQUITY

Gray's Inn in London was perhaps the most famous of the Inns of Court, those uniquely English institutions formed by groups of lawyers to provide an education in law for would-be barristers. Thomas Cromwell, among others, had studied at Gray's. It was here that Thomas Helwys, son of Edmund Helwys of Broxtowe Hall in Nottinghamshire, came to study in the year 1593. He remained here for about two years, long enough to secure an introduction to English common law. Helwys' stay at Gray's was cut short by his marriage to Joan Ashmore of Bilborough Parish in 1595.

During the next few years, Helwys became closely associated with John Smyth, who was a frequent guest in Helwys' rapidly growing household. Joan Helwys was apparently as much committed to the Separatist way as was her husband, for in July 1607 she was arrested and imprisoned in York Castle for violating the Conventicle Act. Apparently her husband escaped similar treatment because he and the Gainsborough Separatists had already left England for Amsterdam. In fact, according to John Robinson, Helwys was the one most insistent on leaving England: "The truth is, it was Mr. Helwisse, who above all, either guides or others, furthered this passage into strange countries: and if any brought oars, he brought sails, as I could show in many particulars, and as all that were acquainted with the manner of our coming over, can witness with me."[1]

But Helwys' enthusiasm for this change waned relatively quickly. John Smyth's death may have triggered Helwys' resolve to return to England, but there were other factors that reinforced his decision. In fact, as early as 1610 Helwys may have reached the conclusion that the Separatists' exodus from England was ill-conceived. Perhaps he never thought of the self-imposed exile in the Netherlands as permanent, a possibility suggested by the fact that there is no evidence that his wife and children ever joined him there. Besides, he had become convinced that he and his followers, as Christ's church, must return to England to bear witness to the truth. To further add to his discomfiture was news from England that two individuals accused of Anabaptism had been put to death for heresy. Bartholomew Legate, a cloth merchant who had been in contact with certain Mennonite groups in the Netherlands, was burned at the stake at St. Paul's in March 1612; in April, Edward Wightman was convicted on similar charges and burned to death at Lichfield. Helwys' sense of guilt must have increased with every fresh account of these tragic events. And, with the death of Smyth, he doubtless felt that a chapter in his own pilgrimage had come to a close. It was time for a new beginning. Besides, nothing more could be gained by further delay.

1. *The Works of John Robinson*, vol. 3 (London: John Snow, 1851), p. 159.

When he returned to England with possibly ten others, Helwys established the first Baptist church on English soil, a fact which can be documented. It was by no means the same church in faith and practice that John Smyth had led to Amsterdam in 1607/1608, nor was it identical to that of the Mennonites with whom the Baptists shared so much common ground. At Spitalfield (Spittlefields), a small group of earnest souls gathered to worship, which represented something new under the English sun.

Like the Marian exiles a half century before, these returning exiles immediately made their presence felt. During his Dutch sojourn Helwys apparently had written a little book entitled *A Short Declaration of the Mistery of Iniquity*, which may have been printed in the Netherlands. (If this is true, then it is further confirmation that Helwys had planned to return to his native land in order to share his newfound faith with his countrymen.) Shortly after his return, Helwys inscribed a copy and sent it to the king. In his inscription Helwys reminded the king of his mortality and the limitations of his royal authority: "The king is a mortall man & not God, therefore hath no power over ye immortal Soules of his Subjects, to make lawes and ordinances for them, and to set Spiritual Lords over them." Helwys went on to remind James that although he was a king, he was not God. He also pledged his obedience to the king "in all thinges," even unto death.[2]

If King James ever read the book, he must have found it as curious as it was objectionable. Within its pages Helwys compared the major religious bodies of his day with the four beasts of Revelation. In a broadside, he condemned the Roman Catholic Church, the Church of England, the Puritans, and the Separatists—in that order. Yet the remarkable thing about *The Mistery of Iniquity* was not its polemics, which were characteristic of the times, or its brash and unpolished style, but the fact that in spite of his strong aversion for those whose teachings he condemned, Helwys argued for complete religious freedom for

2. Helwys, *The Mistery of Iniquity* (Oxford: Bodleian Library; rpt. London: Kingsgate Press, 1935), p. xxiv.

all those so categorized and for others as well—specifically, Roman Catholics, Turks, and Jews.[3]

> We still pray for our Lord the King that wee be free from suspect. For haeving anie thoughts of provoking evill against them of the Romish religion in regard of their profession, if they be true & faithful subjects to the king for wee do freely professe, that our lord the King hath no more power over their consciences then over ours, and that is none at all: for our lord the King is but an earthly King, and he hath no authority as a king can require no more: for mens religion to God is betwixt God and themselves; the King shall not answere for it, neither may the King be jugd betweene God and man. Let them be heretikes, Turcks, Jewes or whatsoever, it apperteynes not to the earthly power to punish them in the least measure.[4]

Such a bold declaration of the principle of religious freedom and the limitation of the king's authority in religious matters could hardly have evoked from an individual of James' perspective anything other than total rejection. Here was something he had doubtless never encountered before. Unlike the Millenary Petition, *The Mistery of Iniquity* made no demands to be acted upon by the king as head of the Church of England. Its author did not, like a whimpering child, even ask the king to grant religious toleration to a despised and suspected sect. Instead, the author warned the king not to sin against God by denying that which God had ordained for all humankind: a relationship with God that was both personal and voluntary. Yet coupled with this bold declaration was the pledge of obedience to all civil laws of the kingdom.

Helwys' patience with the inequities of English law was sorely tried in the crucible of his own experience. Apparently he was arrested early in 1613. Sometime later, possibly in 1614, a petition was sent to Parliament which, according to Champlin Burrage, was in Helwys' handwriting. The petition pointed out

3. Jews had been expelled from England in 1290 and had not been readmitted. Catholics had suffered many hardships, but restrictions were being removed provided they would take the oath of allegiance to the king.
4. Helwys, *The Mistery of Iniquity*, p. 69.

that Roman Catholic recusants who had taken an oath of allegiance to the king had been released from prison, but that neither the writer nor any of his fellow prisoners had been similarly treated:

> But when wee fall under the handes of the Bishops wee can have no benifitt by the said oath, for they say it belongeth onely to Popish recuzantes, & not to others; but kept have wee bene by them many yeres in lingering imprisonmentes, devided from wives, children, servantes & callings, not for any other cause but onely for conscience towardes God, to the utter undoeing of us, our wives & children. Our most humble Supplication therefore to this high & Honorable assemblie is, that in commiseration of the distressed estate of us our poore wives & children it may be enacted in expresse wordes that other [of] the kinges maiesties faithfull subjectes, as well as Popish Recuzantes may be freed from imprisonmentes upon taking the said oath.[5]

Despite the revelation that the prisoners were willing to take an oath of allegiance to the king and the government and that they prayed "night and day" for parliament, the petition was denied. Indeed, it appears never to have gotten out of committee, for on the letter itself is the notation "rejected by the committee."

In the end, Helwys' bold witness cost him his life. (Apparently he had anticipated this consequence, but his convictions would not permit him to act otherwise.) Helwys died in prison sometime before 1616, when his will was probated. But he had accomplished his purpose: he had succeeded in sowing the seeds of religious liberty in England and shaping the basic principles of General Baptist faith and order. Others who would come after him were in his debt for blazing the trail that they attempted to follow.

5. Burrage, *The Early English Dissenters in the Light of Recent Research (1550-1641)*, 2 vols. (1912; repr. New York: Russell & Russell, 1967), 2: 215-16. Burrage notes that this is an early English Baptist petition probably written in 1614, possibly authored by Thomas Helwys.

MARK LEONARD BUSHER AND *RELIGION'S PEACE*

Little is known about Mark Leonard Busher. He appears to have been a citizen of London who, according to his own admission, sought refuge in the Netherlands for the sake of his conscience. In his work of 1612 entitled *Profane Schism,* Christopher Lawne indicated that Busher was the leader of a third congregation of "English Anabaptists." In 1642 Busher was living in the Dutch city of Delft and in contact with the Flemish Mennonites in Amsterdam. He also maintained ties with the English General Baptists while he was still in Holland. His importance to the cause of religious freedom lay in his remarkable book, published the same year in which the petition that Helwys apparently authored was sent to the House of Commons. The book was entitled *Religion's Peace: Or A Plea for Liberty of Conscience,* "presented to King James, and the High Court of Parliament then sitting by Leonard Busher Citizen of London, and printed in the Yeare 1614." It was reprinted in 1646, the year in which the Westminster Confession was published. The reprint contained an additional preface addressed to "the Presbyterian Reader" written by Henry Burton on behalf of the Baptists, who feared the consequences of a Presbyterian-dominated parliament.

The original book consisted of almost seventy pages of closely reasoned arguments for religious liberty supported by numerous Scripture references and quotations. The work was divided into two parts: the first was a long preface of eleven pages addressed to King James; the second, the heart of the book, consisted of fifty-four pages entitled "Certain Reasons Against Persecution." In addition to the arguments advanced by the Continental Anabaptists, Smyth, and Helwys, Busher introduced what could be called sociological arguments. He contended that religious liberty is best for society; persecution, on the other hand, will ultimately destroy any government that practices it: "Therefore persecution for differences in religion is a monstrous and cruel beast, that destroyeth both prince and people, hindereth the gospel of Christ, and scattereth his disciples that witness and profess his name. But permission of

55

conscience in difference of religion, saveth both prince and people."[6]

While Busher extolled the virtues of religious freedom for both church and state, his arguments were basically theological, not political. True religion, he affirmed, is the natural attribute not of birth but of "the new birth," which can never be the result of coercion. "Fire and sword are wholly against the mind and merciful law of Christ,"[7] he wrote; therefore, "no king nor bishop can or is able to command faith."[8] Neither can error be destroyed by fire and sword. In light of these facts, Busher argued that only the separation of church and state provides an adequate solution to the deplorable situation brought about by the state's attempt to usurp the prerogatives of God: "Kings and magistrates are to rule temporal affairs by the swords of their temporal kingdoms, and bishops and ministers are to rule spiritual affairs by the word and Spirit of God, the sword of Christ's spiritual kingdom, and not to intermeddle one with another's authority, office, and function."[9]

In Busher's view, religious freedom, which was based upon the freedom every Christian has in Christ, did not free the Christian from "the moral and judicial law of God." After declaring that Christ has set us free from the traditional ecclesiastical "laws and ordinances" as well as those of the Old Testament, he asserted,

> But he hath not set us free from the moral and judicial law of God; for that the king is bound to execute, and we are bound to obey: and for want of the execution thereof, there are in our land many whores and whore keepers, and many children murdered, besides the death and undoing of many persons about whores. Wherefore, I humbly desire, that the moral and judicial law of God, may be practised and executed on all

6. Busher, *Religion's Peace: Or a Plea for Liberty of Conscience*, in *Tracts on Liberty of Conscience and Persecution: 1614-1661*, ed. Edward Bean Underhill (London: Hanserd Knollys Society, 1846), p. 41.

7. Ibid., p. 16.

8. Ibid., p. 19.

9. Ibid., p. 23.

degrees, both high and low, without respect of persons according to the mind of Christ.[10]

Obviously Busher did not limit the state's jurisdiction when it came to matters of social consequence rooted in immorality. Accordingly, his plea for religious liberty and limitations of the state in religious affairs did not imply a lack of concern either for social problems or for an orderly society in which all citizens might live in peace with justice. In fact, Busher spelled out how England could maintain just such a society without fear of anarchy. He listed seven rules by which those suspected of treason could be kept under surveillance and seditious activities could be contained. He also pointed out that the persecution of dissenters from the established church forced otherwise good and upright citizens to despise the government and hate the king.

In the preface addressed to King James, Busher attempted to dispel the notion that his plea for freedom was a sectarian one which all minorities would not be adverse to making. It is clear that he, like Smyth, believed that Christianity was not limited by sacrament, liturgy, or creed—only by one's personal relationship to Christ:

> Your majesty and parliament shall understand, that all those *that confess,* freely, without compulsion, *that Jesus is the Messiah,* the Lord, *and that he came in flesh,* are to be esteemed the children of God and true Christians seeing such are *born of God;* and *no man can say that Jesus is the Lord, but by the Holy Ghost,* therefore not to be persecuted.[11]

Busher argued for freedom not only for Christians but also for Jews. He asked that they be readmitted to England with full religious and civil liberties. He claimed that such a policy would be good for England as well as for the Jewish people.[12]

Busher's relationship to the English Baptists is not clear, although he was apparently the first among them to insist that

10. Ibid., p. 67.
11. Ibid., pp. 20-21.
12. Ibid., pp. 59ff.

baptism should be by immersion.[13] There is no question that he considered himself a part of the movement with which he had many personal ties, even though he may never have returned to England. (He apparently spent the remainder of his life in the Netherlands.) However, during his lifetime he carried on correspondence with both the English Baptists and the Dutch Mennonites. From this correspondence we learn that even though he was a man of scholarly gifts with a command of Latin, Dutch, and Greek, he lived out his life in poverty.

It is possible that Busher had greater influence among the English Baptists after his death than during his life. The fact that *Religion's Peace* was published in a new edition with a new preface in the very same year in which the Westminster Confession was published would tend to suggest this possibility.

JOHN MURTON AND
OBJECTIONS: ANSWERED BY WAY OF DIALOGUE

John Murton was a young man of only eighteen or nineteen when he accompanied Smyth and Helwys on their exodus from England. Murton sided with Helwys in his dispute with Smyth over the validity of Smyth's self-baptism, and returned to London with Helwys in 1612. With Helwys' imprisonment and death, the mantle of Murton's pastor and friend fell upon him. Thus, although Murton was not more than twenty-five or twenty-six and was a furrier by trade, he became a vigorous and effective champion of the cause.

Murton wrote at least three books setting forth his understanding of law, religious freedom, the separation of church and state, and the distinctive doctrines of the General Baptists. The first of these was entitled *Objections: Answered by Way of Dialogue, wherein is proved By the Law of God: By the Law of our Land: And by King James his many Testimonies, That no*

13. Ibid., p. 59.

man ought to be Persecuted for his Religion, so he Testifie his Allegiance by the Oath appointed by Law. This work was published in 1615 and again in 1662, the second time with a shortened title: *Persecution for Religion Judg'd and Condemn'd.* This edition also included a second booklet attributed to Murton entitled *An Humble Supplication to the King's Majesty,* which was apparently first published in 1620. That these two small books were both influential and representative of the English Baptist position on religious liberty is suggested by the fact that they were reprinted in 1662 and again in 1846.

Murton wrote *Objections* to refute John Robinson's book entitled *Of Religious Communion, Private and Public,* published in 1614. Even though Robinson was a Separatist and the pastor of the Leyden church from which the Pilgrim fathers came, he defended both infant baptism and the magistrate's authority to judge and punish in religious matters. Murton contended that while the magistrates' authority must be obeyed, it extends properly only to civil affairs. In the introduction to *Objections* he wrote,

> We do unfeignedly acknowledge the authority of earthly magistrates, God's blessed ordinance, and that all earthly authority and command appertains unto them; let them command what they will, we must obey, either to do or suffer upon pain of God's displeasure, besides their punishment: but all men must let God alone with his right, which is to be lord and lawgiver to the soul, and not command obedience for God where he commandeth none.[14]

Murton presented his arguments in the form of a dialogue between two individuals called Christian and Antichristian. Repeatedly he had Christian insist that faith cannot be coerced. In one exchange after Christian had affirmed his allegiance to the "king's law," he had Christian say, "But my soul, wherewith I am to worship God, that belongeth to another King, *whose kingdom is not of this world;* whose people must come willingly;

---

14. Murton, *Objections,* in *Tracts on Liberty of Conscience and Persecution,* p. 100.

whose weapons *are not carnal, but spiritual.*"[15] Throughout the work Murton emphasized the dichotomy between the kingdom of this world and the kingdom of God.

In answer to Antichristian's contention that all subjects of the kingdom are bound to obey the "princes," Murton had Christian say, "Most true it is, but is it not also true that princes must afford all their subjects justice and equity, although they be as heathens and publicans?" For Murton insisted that princes are not a law unto themselves but must themselves obey a higher law, the Law of Christ: "is not that law of Christ herein to be observed, that *whatsoever ye would men should do to you, even so do you to them?*"[16] Murton believed that there is no hierarchy of relationships with God. The king could not answer to God on behalf of his people and the people answer to the king; each individual must answer to God not only in regard to his faith but also for the way he treats his neighbor and discharges his responsibilities before God. According to Murton, the secular authorities are accountable for their own faith but also for ruling justly, which includes providing for the freedom that the gospel and an uncoerced faith demand. It is neither the prerogative nor the responsibility of a ruler to judge the truth or error of his subjects' faith or lack of it. This judgment belongs only to God. Throughout this work Murton drove home his point by referring to the parable of the wheat and the tares found in Matthew 13:24-30.

Murton's second work, *An Humble Supplication to the King's Majesty*, was in the form of a petition addressed to parliament, King James, and his son, Prince Charles. Even though this book set forth the same arguments that *Objections* had given for religious freedom and for limiting the magistracy in religious affairs, it was better organized than the previous work. The thesis of *An Humble Supplication* is found in the tenth chapter, in which Murton quoted King James' own words from a speech he delivered at the opening of Parliament in 1620—a speech which the king repeatedly contradicted by his

15. Ibid., p. 108.
16. Ibid., p. 116.

actions. Apparently, after reflecting upon Helwys' earlier work, King James at last came to recognize the truth of the handwritten inscription some seven years after the author's death:

> The wisdom of God foresaw, that seeing the mysteries of the gospel are such spiritual things, as no natural men, though they be princes of this world, can know them; he left not kings and princes to be lords and judges thereof, seeing they are subject to err. But he left that power to his beloved Son, who could not err; and the Son left his only deputy, the Holy Ghost, and no mortal man whatsoever; as your highness worthily acknowledgeth, in [your] Apology.[17]

Unfortunately, Murton was to meet the same fate as Helwys. According to W. T. Whitley, Murton was jailed because of his faith, spending about ten years in Newgate Prison. He proved to be an able and dedicated leader among the Baptists during this time, until his death in 1530. Evidence of his influence may be seen not only in his works, of which there may have been as many as five, but also in the spread of the movement. By 1626 there were five such congregations in correspondence with the Waterlander Mennonites, with whom they attempted to establish closer ties. These overtures came to naught, however. The Waterlanders renewed correspondence in 1630, upon which occasion Murton's widow left England for Holland, where she joined the English branch of the Waterlander Mennonite church. By this time there were at least eight Baptist churches in England, mainly in Kent and Essex counties.

While the influence of John Murton and the General Baptists[18] may have been negligible as far as the king and parliament

---

17. Murton, *An Humble Supplication*, in *Tracts on Liberty of Conscience and Persecution*, p. 227.

18. The General Baptists were the first Baptists. They were known first as Anabaptists, a term which they rejected. Later they were called General Baptists because they held to a concept of general atonement: they believed that Christ died for all individuals of whatever race, sex, and nation (but they also believed that only those who freely put their trust in him were saved). In contrast, the Particular Baptists were so named because they held that Christ died for the elect alone. See A. C. Underwood, *A History*

were concerned, these little-known and despised people had succeeded in introducing into England the concept of religious freedom with responsibility. Anyone who had been willing to take the time to investigate this group would have discovered that these advocates of freedom were Englishmen who, while insisting upon religious freedom for themselves, argued for no less for all others. Most did not even deny the government the use of the sword or object to taking an oath of allegiance to the king, and they were willing to admit to their churches a magistrate who gave evidence of having genuinely experienced salvation. However, they did deny the magistracy any jurisdiction in religious matters, and they insisted upon justice and equality before the law, both of which they failed to receive. But the seed had been sown and would in time produce a harvest.

PARTICULAR BAPTISTS AND THE ENGLISH GOVERNMENT

The Particular Baptists arose out of an Independent Puritan conventicle that was formed in London by Henry Jacob in 1616. Jacob had returned from the Netherlands only a short time before. A number of secessions from the original congregation occurred, which eventually led the splinter groups as well as the original church to adopt believer's baptism by immersion. One of the major differences between this new Baptist development and the older Baptist movement was that these Baptists, like most Englishmen, were Calvinists in soteriology—though not strict Calvinists. Theirs was a modified Calvinism that said nothing about reprobation; hence they held to single rather than double predestination. The First London Confession of 1644 and a revised edition of 1646 put even more distance between them and other Separatists. By 1646, the articles on the magistracy, which detailed its authority and the limitations of that authority

of the English Baptists (London: Carey Kingsgate Press Limited, 1947), pp. 28-55.

which made possible religious freedom, were greatly expanded and made much more explicit. A brief comparison of the confession of 1644 with the 1646 edition will illustrate the point.

Article XLVIII of the First London Confession of 1644 acknowledged that "a civil Magistracie is an ordinance of God" which must be obeyed "in all lawfull things." It enjoined all to pray for the king. Article XLIX explained that those who adhered to this confession acknowledged that the "supreme Magistracie of this Kingdome we beleeve to be the King and Parliament freely chosen by the Kingdome." The confession went on to declare that the seven churches issuing it felt "bound to defend both the persons of those thus chosen, and all civil Lawes made by them," with everything they had, including their very lives. They declared, "Although we should suffer never so much from them in not actively submitting to some Ecclesiasticall Lawes, which might be conceived by them to be their duties to establish which we for the present could not see, nor our consciences could submit unto; yet are we bound to yeeld our persons to their pleasures."[19]

In 1646 the Westminster Assembly met and drew up a confession by that name. From all appearances the Presbyterians were about to take over the whole government and impose their church upon the entire nation. Understandably, the Baptists were uneasy. In·response to the threat they perceived and the increasingly virulent attacks upon them by their enemies, including a certain polemical Presbyterian divine by the name of Dr. Daniel Featley, the Baptists in 1646 published a new edition of their earlier confession, making a number of modifications. For one thing, instead of setting forth a fourfold ministry for the local church, this edition, following the pattern of the General Baptists, recognized only pastors and deacons. In addition, the articles on the magistracy and religious free-

19. *Baptist Confessions of Faith*, ed. William L. Lumpkin (Philadelphia: Judson Press, 1959), p. 169. This confession was sent out in the name of "the contemned [condemned] Churches of Christ in London." The title given the confession was "The Confession of Faith, of those Churches which are commonly (though falsly) called Anabaptists." However, the confession became known as the First London Confession.

dom were both strengthened and expanded, and Article XXXVIII became XLVIII. After expressing their gratitude for the apparent disestablishment of the Anglican Church, they declared,

> And concerning the worship of God; there is but one lawgiver, which is able to save and destroy, *James 4:12*; which is Jesus Christ, who hath given laws and rules sufficient in His word for His worship. . . . So it is the magistrates duty to tender the liberty of mens' consciences, *Eccles. 8:8* (which is the tenderest thing unto all conscientious men, and most dear unto them, and without which all other liberties will not be worth the naming, much less enjoying) and to protect all under them from all wrong, injury, oppression and molestation; so it is our duty not to be wanting in nothing which is for their honor and comfort, and whatsoever is for the well-being of the commonwealth wherein we live; it is our duty to do, and we believe it to be our express duty, especially in matters of religion, to be fully persuaded in our minds of the lawfulness of what we do, as knowing whatsoever is not of faith is sin. And as we cannot do anything contrary to our understandings and consciences, so neither can we forbear the doing of that which our understandings and consciences bind us to do.[20]

Article XLIX reinforced the willingness of those issuing the confession to die for their faith rather than compromise that which they held to be the clear teachings of Scripture. They also added a completely new article—Article L, in which they stated a Christian could be a "magistrate or civil officer." They also

---

20. "A Confession of Faith of Seven Congregations or Churches of Christ in London, which are Commonly (but unjustly) Called Anabaptists" (London: Printed by *Matth. Simmons*, And Are To Be Sold By *John Hancock* in Popes-Head Alley, 1646; repr. Rochester, N.Y.: Backus Book Publishers, 1981), pp. 17-18. This article spells out the government's (magistrates') responsibility to provide religious liberty, which is, according to this confession, the basic freedom. This indicates that the concept of religious liberty and the concept of a government limited to civil matters only, ideas introduced into England by the General Baptists (who were considered Arminian), were now firmly a part of the life and thought of Calvinistic Baptists. The concept of religious liberty would eventually win adherents among other Calvinists as well.

stated their position on oaths, declaring that an oath could be taken "for the confirmation of truth," but that frivolous and vain oaths were prohibited.

The confession was brought to a close with a ringing affirmation of their faith and the rights of individual conscience. These Baptists reaffirmed their determination to obey civil authority while at the same time declaring their resolve "to die a thousand deaths, rather than to doe any thing against the least tittle of the truth of God, or against the light of our own consciences. And if any shall call what we have said Heresie, then doe we with the Apostle acknowledge, that after the way they call heresie, worship we the God of our Fathers."[21]

This confession proved to be one of the most influential of the early Baptist confessions. New editions were published in 1651 and again in 1652. An edition entitled "A Fifth Impression Corrected" appeared in 1653. There may have been still other editions, and there were numerous reprints. All of this indicates that for more than a century this confession was useful in expressing Baptists' understanding of the Christian faith. Even when the Second London Confession, which was based largely on the Westminster Confession of 1646, was adopted by the Particular Baptists, it retained phrases from the First London Confession (1646 edition) and added an article—Article XXI on religious liberty—which utilized phrases reminiscent of both Smyth and Murton. In fact, there is no Baptist confession, Calvinistic or otherwise, of which I am aware that fails to include an article on religious liberty and the limitations of the state's authority in religious matters.

SAMUEL RICHARDSON AND *THE NECESSITY OF TOLERATION IN MATTERS OF RELIGION*

By 1644 a number of voices had begun to advocate toleration and religious freedom. This was the year in which Roger Wil-

21. Ibid., p. 20.

liams emerged from the American wilderness to publish *The Bloudy Tenent of Persecution*. Aside from Williams and John Milton, both of whom argued for religious freedom, Samuel Richardson was the most significant person to speak on behalf of religious liberty. He was a wealthy London merchant who was among the signers of the Particular Baptist confessions of faith of 1643, 1644, and 1646. That he was a recognized leader among the English Baptists is indicated by his reply to Dr. Daniel Featley's scurrilous attack upon the Baptists, a reply he entitled *Some Brief Considerations on Doctor Featley His book entitled The Dippers Dipt*. In addition to this work, Richardson wrote between ten and eleven other books. Unlike some of his Baptist colleagues, he was an ardent supporter of Oliver Cromwell. W. K. Jordan noted that although Richardson had his reservations about Cromwell, his attitude toward him was in many ways positive. "He shared the normal Baptist aversion to the formality of the Cromwellian settlement of religion and viewed with disapproval the conservative political tendencies which led to the establishment of the Protectorate. But as a prudent and responsible leader, Richardson was gravely alarmed by the violence of the attacks which were launched against the Protectorate by Fifth Monarchy and other radical writers."[22]

Richardson's importance for our study lies in his advocacy of religious liberty and the limitations of the state in matters of religion as set forth in his *Necessity of Toleration in Matters of Religion*. This work was called forth by the Westminster Assembly of 1646, and was published the following year. The author introduced his subject by reproducing what he titled "The Imperial Constitution of Constantinus and Licinius." Next he stated the five principles of religious freedom upon which he based questions addressed to the Presbyterians who wished to establish the Scottish Presbyterian system in England. These were followed by a succinct, twelve-point statement of the Westminster Assembly's position on the use of parliament to advance its cause. This section was then followed by a list of thirteen reasons why

22. Jordan, cited by Underwood in *A History of the English Baptists*, p. 80.

Nonconformists, according to Richardson, could not submit to such a system. A conclusion summed up the Baptists' adamant opposition to a Presbyterian establishment of religion.

A few excerpts from *The Necessity of Toleration* will convey the tenor of the book. The first of the five principles about why religion is not subject to coercion is this: "Because it is God's way to have religion free, and only to flow from an inward principle of faith and love, neither would God be worshipped of unwilling worshippers." The third point says that the church must be separated from the world in order to bear an authentic Christian witness in the world. The fifth point emphasizes that freedom of religion is best for society because it makes possible a government by which all are treated alike and each person learns to live in mutual toleration of others who may not share the same confessional stance.[23]

An example of the kinds of questions Richardson posed to the Presbyterians is question 56:

> Whether it be not a horrible thing that a free division of England may not have so much liberty as is permitted to a Turk in this kingdom: who, although he denies Christ, yet he can live quietly amongst us here? And is it not a great ingratitude of this kingdom to deny this liberty to such as are friends, and have been a means in their persons and estates to save this kingdom from destruction and desolation? Oh, England, England! Oh that thou wert wise to know the things that belong to thy prosperity and peace, before it be too late! The hand of God is against thee. How have we slain one another; and who knows but this is come upon us for troubling, undoing, despising, and banishing the people of God into so many wildernesses?[24]

In the conclusion of his book, Richardson rebuked the Westminster divines for calling "persecution discipline and just deserved censure" and instead called them to follow the Golden Rule of Christ. There is the suggestion that Richardson believed that the Presbyterians were incapable of mounting any compre-

23. Richardson, *The Necessity of Toleration*, in *Tracts on Liberty of Conscience and Persecution*, pp. 253-54.
24. Ibid., p. 265.

hensive policy of persecution against the Nonconformists due to Cromwell's opposition. This did in fact prove to be the case. It was the New Model Army, however, that defeated the plan of the Presbyterian-dominated parliament to set up a new state church. As A. C. Underwood expressed it, "Independents and Baptists formed the backbone of the New Model Army. They were not impressed men but volunteers and they were determined to secure the religious liberty for which they had fought. Having thrown off the tyranny of [Archbishop] Laud, they were not prepared to submit to another."[25]

THE NEW MODEL ARMY AND RELIGIOUS LIBERTY

The New Model Army refused to enter the new state church that parliament had established. Cromwell was sympathetic. The Nonconformists—Baptists and Independents—had served Cromwell well and constituted a significant power base for him. When they rejected the new state church, Cromwell determined to maintain the Anglican Church but without bishops. For the purpose of bringing order out of chaos, he appointed a body of triers who were responsible for assessing the clergy's intellectual, moral, and spiritual fitness. A. C. Underwood points out that "in the ministry of the state church he did not scruple to include Presbyterians, Independents, and Baptists, while leaving untouched non-royalist Anglicans, provided they were qualified for their office and did not use the Prayer Book."[26] The Baptists' response to Cromwell's creation was mixed. Of the thirty-eight central triers appointed in 1654, six were Baptists. A few other Baptists accepted state-paid

25. Underwood, *A History of the English Baptists*, p. 64. The New Model Army was created by Cromwell. As Underwood points out, it was made up largely of Independents (Congregationalists) and Baptists. Officers were promoted from the ranks; promotion was based on performance and not one's position in the British aristocracy.
26. Ibid., p. 65.

appointments in the established church, but the majority saw the inconsistency of becoming a part of any established church, regardless of the freedom it granted. In 1656 the Western Association, which was made up of Particular Baptist churches centered in the area from the western part of England to the Bristol Channel, published a circular letter that articulated Baptist opposition to Cromwell's scheme:

> We answer that a Preacher of the Gospel ought not to accept the place of Minister to a Parish, or Lecturer, or Champlain, not to take a set maintenance of the world for preaching the Word. . . . It stops the mouth of a Minister from bearing an open and full testimony against the practice of the Parish Ministry, who, Balaam-like, run after the reward; and seeing this is the way of Anti-Christ's Ministers, it becometh not Christ's thus to follow the reward, whither that goeth, thither to go.[27]

Some Baptists became so disillusioned with Cromwell when he set up the Protectorate and assumed the title of Lord Protector that they became a part of the Fifth Monarchy movement. The Fifth Monarchists derived their name from the prophet Daniel's vision described in Daniel 2. They fervently believed that Christ would return soon to establish his millennial kingdom. (Indeed, England was filled with such expectations.) Thus the Fifth Monarchists were disappointed by Cromwell's assumption of kingly authority, and they decided to take matters into their own hands. Led by Major General Thomas Harrison, they attempted armed intervention to prepare for the second advent of Christ. They failed: the movement was crushed by Cromwell. All denominations except the Presbyterians were involved, but the Baptists suffered the most. Their relationship with the Fifth Monarchists proved an unmitigated disaster, because Baptists were once again associated with mindless revolutionaries.[28] The Baptists who were a part of this movement and survived became Seventh-Day Baptists.

27. Cited by Underwood in ibid., p. 81.
28. In opposition to the Fifth Monarchists, Samuel Richardson compromised his previous position on religious liberty, which also proved

THE ENGLISH BAPTIST HERITAGE

Despite a momentary setback, English Baptists emerged at the end of the seventeenth century a vital force on the religious scene. Although the brief period during which they enjoyed active participation in the government came to an abrupt end with the return of Charles II to the English throne, they still remained positive about the prospects for their participation in the political process, even though such participation seemed an impossibility, since they were barred from holding public office as well as holding positions in universities, the army, and the fleet.

With the complete restoration of the Church of England and its liturgy and prelates under Charles II, religious persecution became the order of the day. From 1661 to 1665 parliament enacted the Clarendon Code in order to suppress dissent, and dissenters once again became the victims of severe persecution. Unfortunately, early in January 1661 Thomas Venner, a Fifth Monarchy man who was a wine cooper by trade, invaded London with fifty followers; they killed twenty-two people in the name of God and the Fifth Monarchy movement. As a result, on January 10, 1661, a royal proclamation prohibited all meetings of "Anabaptists, Quakers, and Fifth Monarchy men."[29] By 1662, some 4,230 Quakers and 289 "Anabaptists" and others had been thrown into prison.[30] In 1664, twelve General Baptists were sentenced to die for refusing to abide by an act of 1593 against dissenters. The twelve were saved from execution at the last minute by a royal pardon.[31] John James, a

---

detrimental to Baptists as did *The Torments of Hell,* a book attributed to him. See Paul Linton Gritz, "Samuel Richardson and the Religious and Political Controversies Confronting the London Particular Baptists, 1643 to 1658," Ph.D. diss., Southwestern Baptist Theological Seminary, 1987.

29. Michael R. Watts, *The Dissenters: From the Reformation to the French Revolution,* vol. 1 (Oxford: Oxford University Press, 1978), p. 223.

30. Ibid.

31. Thomas Crosby, *The History of the English Baptists,* vol. 2 (1738; repr. Lafayette, Tenn.: Church History Research and Archives, 1979), pp. 180-85. It was during this period of renewed persecution that John Bunyan was imprisoned at Bedford.

Seventh-Day Baptist preacher at Whitechapel, was not so fortunate. Although the evidence against him was dubious, he was executed for treason. Finally, in 1689, the Act of Toleration brought a measure of relief, although complete religious liberty was never achieved in England.

Despite restrictions under which all Nonconformists were forced to live, English Baptists continued to increase and make a number of significant contributions to Christendom and the world. Among these, the concepts of religious liberty and the institutional separation of church and state may be the most significant. Although these principles were never completely implemented in England, they were to find a lodging place in a new land and eventually play a most significant role in the birth of the American republic.

---- Chapter IV ----

Conflicting Visions
in Puritan New England

The shores of the New World beckoned refugees from among Europe's persecuted dissenters like the promised land of ancient Israel's hopes and dreams. The analogy between ancient Israel and New England was obvious to the early colonizers, but it was variously interpreted. It was viewed as providential by the Bay Colony's leading Puritan pastor, Dr. John Cotton. He saw Massachusetts Bay as the New Israel and the Indians as the Amalekites. On the other hand, Roger Williams, the founder of Providence, thought Cotton was dead wrong. Williams saw the New Israel as made up of the people of God—drawn from many different nations, tongues, and races—who had become such by the new birth. Accordingly, he saw the Indians not as the Amalekites but as the objects of God's mercy and grace. As a consequence, he sought to learn their language and cultivate their friendship. These two utterly different visions were bound to collide once Williams discovered for himself the theocratic foundations of the Puritan colony.

Before Williams arrived in the New World, the English had succeeded in establishing three colonies on differing religious foundations. Jamestown was officially Anglican, although some of the early colonists such as Henry Jacob were of the Puritan persuasion. Plymouth, the colony of the Pilgrim fathers, was Separatist, while Massachusetts Bay was strictly non-Separatist Puritan. The colony of Massachusetts Bay as Governor John Winthrop envisioned it was a commercial venture, both English and Puritan. The whole enterprise was bathed in Puritan piety, a fact clearly illustrated by Winthrop's *Modell of Christian Charity*. Winthrop brought his treatise on a Puritan theocracy to a close with these words:

> Therefore lett us choose life,
> that wee, and our Seede,
> may live, by obeyeing his
> voyce, and cleaveing to him,
> for hee is our life and
> our prosperity.[1]

Only two years after Massachusetts Bay Colony had been founded, Roger Williams and his wife, Mary Barnard, arrived in the New World. Williams' reputation for piety and learning had preceded him. He was an ordained Anglican clergyman and a graduate of Pembroke College, Cambridge, where he had been the Charterhouse scholar from 1623 to 1629.[2] He was also a staunch Puritan known for his outspoken opposition to the Book of Common Prayer. Upon his arrival in Lynn (he arrived on February 6, 1631), the First Church of Boston invited him to become the teacher of the church, but he refused on the grounds that the church was made up of "unseparated people." Apparently Williams knew more about the Boston congregation than its members knew about him. It appears that he settled almost immediately in Plymouth, a colony much closer to his own convictions. Two years later he began to serve the church at Salem. While he was here, his outspoken opposition to the assumptions of the Massachusetts Bay Colony brought him into direct conflict with Bay authorities, including Dr. John

1. Winthrop, *A Modell of Christian Charity*, in *Winthrop Papers*, vol. 2: *1623-1630* (Boston: Massachusetts Historical Society, 1931), p. 295.

2. James Ernst, *Roger Williams: New England Firebrand* (New York: Macmillan, 1932), p. 33. Ernst wrote, "He left Pembroke at the end of the sixth term and entered holy orders in December, 1628, or January, 1629."

Cotton, who in 1633 had become the teacher of First Church of Boston.

COTTON'S VISION

Cotton's advocacy of theocracy as the best form of government for colonies in New England fit Massachusetts Bay like a glove. When the Reverend John Davenport sought Cotton's advice about the best government for New Haven, Cotton responded with a carefully delineated exposition of the theocratic ideal:

> Argument 1: Theocracy, or to make the Lord God our governor, is the best form of government in a Christian commonwealth, and . . . men who are free to choose (as in a new plantation they are) ought to establish [it]. . . . That form of government where, (a) the people who have the power of choosing their governors are in covenant with God, (b) wherein the men chosen by them are godly men and fitted with a spirit of government, (c) in which the laws they rule by are the laws of God, (d) wherein laws are executed, inheritances allotted, and civil differences are composed according to God's appointment, [and] (e) in which men of God are consulted [about] all hard cases and in matters of religion, [this] is the form which was received and established among the people of Israel while the Lord God was their governor.[3]

In this work, Cotton's model for New Haven was Israel as it was described in the Old Testament. Cotton went on to indicate that the church is related to the commonwealth as the soul is to the body. In Argument 4 he declared, "That form of government [in which] the power of civil administration is denied unto unbelievers and [is] committed to the saints is the best form of government in a Christian Commonwealth."[4]

---

3. Cotton, "A Discourse about Civil Government," in *Church and State in American History: The Burden of Religious Pluralism*, 2nd rev. ed., ed. John F. Wilson and Donald L. Drakeman (Boston: Beacon Press, 1987), p. 7.
    4. Ibid.

WILLIAMS' OPPOSITION

Williams' concept of the church and consequently of the relationship of the state to the church was completely different from that of Dr. John Cotton and his fellow Puritans. This can be seen in virtually everything Williams ever wrote, but no more clearly than in his *Queries of Highest Consideration*, published in 1644 and "Addressed to the Dissenting Brethren and the Scottish Commissioners at the Westminster Assembly in London." In this treatise he raised several questions about the attempt to make the Presbyterian Church the established church of the land. It is evident in this document that Williams drew his ideas from the New Testament rather than the Old. In Query IV he questioned the validity of the concept of a church that embraces all citizens of a given country:

> Query IV. Whether in your consciences before God you be not persuaded—notwithstanding your promiscuous joining with all—that few of the people of England and Scotland (and fewer of the nobles and gentry) are such spiritual matter, living stones, truly regenerate and converted? And therefore whether it be not the greatest courtesy in the world which you may possibly perform unto them to acquaint them impartially with their condition and how impossible it is for a dead stone to have fellowship with the living God, and for any man to enter the kingdom of God without a second birth? John 3.[5]

Williams then proceeded to question the biblical basis for a state church. Although the Westminster Assembly was the target of this particular arrow, no doubt Williams also had John Cotton and Massachusetts Bay in mind:

> Query VII. We query where you now find one footstep, print, or pattern in this doctrine of the Son of God for a national holy covenant and so, consequently, . . . a national church? Where find you evidence of a whole nation, country or kingdom converted to the faith, and of Christ's appointing of a whole

---

5. Williams, *Queries of Highest Consideration*, in *Church and State in American History: The Burden of Religious Pluralism*, p. 9.

nation or kingdom to walk in one way of religion?

Again we ask whether . . . the constitution of a national church . . . can possibly be framed without a racking and tormenting of souls as well as of the bodies of persons, for it seems not possible to fit it to every conscience?[6]

After calling attention to the Netherlands, where toleration was practiced as far more pleasing to God and nearer the teachings of the New Testament than the practices of Massachusetts, Williams, in one of the most eloquent passages in any of his works, argued forcefully against the assumption that Israel was a legitimate model for church-state relations:

We know the allegations against this counsel [of mine]: the [archetype of such practice] is from Moses (not Christ), his pattern is the typical land of Canaan, the kings of Israel and Judah, &c. We believe [that this] will be found [to be] but one of Moses' shadows which vanished at the coming of the Lord Jesus—yet such a shadow as is directly opposite to the very testament and coming of the Lord Jesus. [It is] opposite to the very nature of a Christian Church, the only holy nation and Israel of God. [It is] opposite to the very tender bowels of humanity (and how much more Christianity?), [which] abhors to pour out the blood of men merely for their souls' belief and worship. [It is] opposite to the Jews conversion to Christ by not permitting them a civil life or being. [It is] opposite to the civil peace and the lives of millions slaughtered upon this ground in mutual persecuting of each other's consciences, especially the Protestant and the Papist. [It is] opposite to the souls of all men who by persecutions are ravished into a dissembled worship which their hearts embrace not. [It is] opposite to the best of God's servants who, in all Popish and Protestant states, have been commonly esteemed and persecuted as the only schismatics, heretics, &c. [It is] opposite to that light of scripture which is expected yet to shine [but] which must, by that doctrine, be suppressed as a new or old heresy or novelty. All this in all ages experience testifies [to], [ages] which never saw any long lived fruit of peace or righteousness grow upon that fatal tree.[7]

6. Ibid.
7. Ibid.

It is not surprising that Plymouth was more to Williams' liking than the Bay, because the Pilgrim fathers were considered true Separatists who had forsaken all in order to worship God according to their own insights and understanding of Scripture. But Williams soon discovered that the Plymouth colonists were no more inclined to tolerate dissenters than the colonists of Massachusetts Bay. Thus, when the opportunity afforded itself, Williams moved to Salem, where the extent of his contentions with the New Israel of Cotton's vision became manifest. It now became quite clear to the colonial authorities that Williams' teachings were subversive and that if he was left alone to propagate his ideas, he would undermine the very foundations of the Puritan theocracy.

Williams was brought to trial and sentenced to be banished from the colony on October 9, 1635. Among the charges brought against him was the charge that he had said that the king of England had no right to grant a charter to Massachusetts Bay because the king was not the rightful owner of the land. He claimed the Indians alone could authorize such a settlement. He also argued that the magistrates had no right to enforce the first four of the Ten Commandments because these pertained to an individual's relationship to God. Therefore, the Bay colony was infringing upon God's prerogative by requiring a uniformity of faith and worship. Williams further irritated both the clergy and the magistrates by denying the colony's identity as the New Israel. The ramifications of this claim troubled Williams' critics. If Massachusetts Bay were not the New Israel, then neither were the Indians the Amalekites, as Dr. John Cotton had claimed. Thus the Puritans had no license to go Indian hunting; instead, they should take the gospel to those who were also the objects of God's mercy. For they too, according to Williams, could be a part of the New Israel, because the New Israel was neither a particular nation nor a particular race but all the regenerate of many races and countries. Accordingly, Williams made this argument in his *Queries of Highest Consideration:*

> Furthermore if the Honourable Houses (the representative commonweal) shall erect a spiritual court for the judging of

spiritual men and spiritual causes (although a new name be put upon it) [we query] whether or not such a court is not in the true nature and kind of it an High Commission? And is not this a reviving of Moses and the sanctifying of a new land of Canaan of which we hear nothing in the Testament of Jesus Christ, nor of any other holy nation but the particular Church of Christ? (I Peter 2:9)

Is not this to subject this holy nation, this heavenly Jerusalem, the wife and spouse of Jesus, the pillar and ground of truth to the uncertain and changeable mutations of this present evil world?[8]

Although Williams wrote his treatise as an open letter to the Westminster Assembly, he had other state churches in mind as well—those of Rome, Scotland, and Massachusetts Bay. Here no less than in *The Bloudy Tenent of Persecution* Williams was setting forth universal principles of church-state relations.

PROVIDENCE

Williams' sentence was not immediately carried out because winter was setting in and Mary, Williams' wife, was pregnant. However, Williams was unable to keep his opinions to himself, something the court had stipulated he do. Warned by Governor Winthrop that plans were afoot to send him back to England, Williams fled into the wilderness, where, after four days of trudging through a blinding snowstorm, he found refuge among the Massasoits. In the spring he purchased some land from the Indians and founded a colony on the Narragansett Bay at the mouth of the Mohassac River. He named it Providence because he was convinced that God had led him there. Soon a number of friends joined him, and together they drew up a compact declaring that the new colony would be governed by the expressed will of the majority but "only in civil things." Thus, by June of 1636, Williams had succeeded in setting up a state

8. Ibid.

providing for complete religious liberty. The compact made it clear that these Englishmen had no intention of disobeying the civil laws of the kingdom. They were not anarchists but deeply religious colonists and partners in the founding of a radically different kind of state—a democracy with absolute freedom in religious matters, as an excerpt from their compact shows:

> We whose names are hereunder written do with free and joint consent promise each unto other that for our common peace and welfare (until we hear further of the King's royal pleasure concerning ourselves) we will from time to time subject ourselves in active and passive obedience to such orders and agreements as shall be made by the greater number of the present house-holders, and such as shall hereafter be admitted by their consent into the same privilege and covenant in our ordinary meeting only in civil things.[9]

Eight years later, Williams was able to secure from the English parliament a charter for his little colony that embodied the principles first enunciated in the compact of 1636. Subsequently, after the collapse of the Commonwealth and the return of Charles II to the English throne, the colonists were able through the efforts of Dr. John Clarke to secure a new charter in 1663. While Williams may have indirectly inspired its composition, in all probability it represents the culmination of efforts made by Clarke, who remained in England for thirteen years to secure the coveted document.[10]

The securing of the first charter virtually guaranteed the legitimacy if not the viability of Rhode Island Colony based upon the principle of religious liberty supported by the separation of church and state. Although despised and denigrated by Massachusetts Bay authorities as the garbage dump of New England and convulsed by internal dissension, the "livelie experiment" survived to set a pattern of democratic government

---

9. Cited by Joseph Martin Dawson in *Baptists and the American Republic* (Nashville: Broadman Press, 1956), p. 34.

10. Ibid., p. 35. See also a letter that John Clarke wrote to Charles II in 1562, reproduced by Thomas W. Bicknell in *Story of Dr. John Clarke* (Providence, R.I.: n.p., 1915), pp. 192-93.

that in time would become characteristic of the new nation in the process of emerging on the shores of the New World.

Although Williams was the guiding genius of Rhode Island, in his lifetime he was harshly criticized by his Puritan adversaries. Cotton Mather claimed that Williams' mind was like a Dutch windmill that turned so fast that eventually it burned itself out. But recent historical commentators praise Williams. The Harvard savant Perry Miller, for example, favorably assesses Williams without making him into a modern man, and comes much closer to the truth than Mather when he writes,

> For the subsequent history of what became the United States, Roger Williams possesses one indubitable importance, that he stands at the beginning of it. Just as some great experience in the youth of a person is ever afterward a determinant of his personality, so the American character has inevitably been molded by the fact that in the first years of colonization there arose this prophet of religious liberty.[11]

Williams also stands at the beginning of the Baptist movement in America. Even though the church that he organized was founded some two years after Providence was established and Williams soon left it to become a Seeker, he never forsook his commitment to religious freedom or the basic insights that made him "the prophet in the wilderness." True enough, it was Dr. John Clarke rather than Williams who lent stability to the movement and aided its spread into other New England communities. Nevertheless, it was Williams' understanding of the primacy of the New Testament that became a major driving force in helping him formulate his views of church-state relations. Other principles of Williams' theology out of which arose his teachings on religious liberty may be gleaned from his writings, the most important of which is *The Bloudy Tenent of Persecution*, which appeared in print on July 15, 1644.

Nominally a Calvinist, Williams embraced hermeneutics similar to those of the sixteenth-century Anabaptists and

---

11. Miller, *Roger Williams: His Contribution to the American Tradition* (New York: Atheneum, 1962), p. 254.

seventeenth-century English General Baptists. Like them, he saw a radical discontinuity between the Old and the New Testament. He held that the Old Testament was never meant to be final or complete—only preparatory and temporal. Accordingly, the New Israel could never be identified with Massachusetts Bay or any other state or nation. Because the New Israel was made up of the "born again," it transcended national and racial divisions. Obviously, Williams saw the New Testament alone as the ultimate authority for the Christian and the church.

From his reading of the New Testament, Williams came to reject the Old World *corpus christianum*. To this ill-conceived union of church and state he attributed the terrible persecutions of the past. According to Williams, the church is made up only of those who voluntarily commit their lives to Christ in faith; hence the church acknowledges the lordship of Christ alone. This means that the state and the church must be separate. Clearly, Williams derived the concept of a secular state from his ecclesiology, not the other way around. At the heart of Williams' view of both the church and the nature of Christian faith was his insistence that faith cannot be coerced. This is a recurring theme throughout all Williams' works:

> Can the sword of steel or arm of flesh make man faithful or loyal to God? Or careth God for the outward loyalty or faithfulness, when the inward man is false and treacherous? Or is there not more danger from a hypocrite, a dissembler, a turncoat in his religion (from the fear or favor of men) than from a resolved Jew, Turk, or papist, who holds firm unto his principles?[12]

Speaking as a Calvinist to Calvinists, Williams drove his point home by reminding his readers that faith itself is a gift of God and not subject to the coercion of men: "Faith is that gift which proceeds alone from the Father of lights, and till he please to make his light arise and open the eyes of blind sinners, their

---

12. Williams, cited by Roland H. Bainton in *The Travail of Religious Liberty* (New York: Harper & Brothers, 1951), pp. 219-20.

souls shall lie fast asleep—and the faster, in that a sword of steel compels them to a worship in hypocrisy."[13]

To his argument about the nature of faith, Williams added a number of other arguments. He insisted that compulsion in matters of religion will not work because diversity is the law of life. Accordingly, pluralism in religion is an irrepressible reality. Moreover, such pluralism is a divine right, because God forces no one to worship him. In addition, Williams pointed out, the state by its very nature is precluded from judging the merits of one's faith. Williams noted that the state's incompetence in this area had been demonstrated time and again by both the Roman Catholic and the Protestant state churches, which had repeatedly mistaken saints for sinners and thus punished thousands of God-fearing and law-abiding citizens. Only God is able to judge between the wheat and the tares, and he has reserved this prerogative for himself. True, the state is ordained by God to serve its God-given function—but that function, according to Williams, is purely secular.

In the introductory argument for writing *The Bloudy Tenent of Persecution*, Williams set forth the principles that he intended to discuss in the book. In the fifth principle he declared, "All *Civill States* with their *Officers* of *justice* in their respective *constitutions* and *administrations* are proved *essentially Civill*, and therefore not *Judges, Governours* or *Defendours* of the *Spirituall* or *Christian state* and *Worship*."[14] In the tenth principle Williams seemed to echo Hubmaier when he wrote, "An inforced *uniformity* of *Religion* throughout a *Nation* or *civill state*, confounds the *Civill* and *Religious*, denies the principles of Christianity and civility, and that *Jesus Christ* is come in the *Flesh*."[15] This may have been Williams' most forceful argument against persecution.

13. Ibid., p. 220.

14. Williams, *The Bloudy Tenent of Persecution*, in *The Complete Writings of Roger Williams*, 7 vols. (New York: Russell & Russell, Inc., 1963), 3:3. See also Williams, *The Bloudy Tenent of Persecution*, in *American Christianity: An Historical Interpretation with Representative Documents*, ed. Shelton H. Smith, Robert T. Handy, and Lefferts A. Loetscher, vol. 1 (New York: Charles Scribner's Sons, 1960), pp. 152-58.

15. Williams, *The Bloudy Tenent of Persecution*, in *The Complete Writings of Roger Williams*, 3:4.

He was saying that to persecute in the name of Christ is in essence to deny the Incarnation. He reinforced this point in Chapter XXXVII, when, in the dialogue between *Peace* and *Truth*, he had *Truth* explain the limitations of even a Christian magistrate's power:

> First, if the *Civill Magistrate* be a *Christian*, a *Disciple* or follower of the meeke *Lambe* of God, he is bound to be far from destroying the *bodies of men*, for refusing to receive the *Lord Jesus Christ*, for otherwise he should not know (according to this speech of the *Lord Jesus*) what *spirit* he was of, yea and to be ignorant of the sweet end of the comming of the Son of Man, which was not to destroy the *bodies of Men*, but to save both *bodies* and *soules*.[16]

The argument continues in this vein:

> Secondly, if the *Civill Magistrate*, being a *Christian*, gifted, *prophesie* in the *Church*, I Corinth. 1.14 although the *Lord Jesus Christ*, whom they in their owne persons hold forth, shall be refused, yet they are here forbidden to call for fire from *heaven*, that is, to procure or inflict any corporall *judgement* upon such *offenders*, remembering the end of the *Lord Jesus* his comming, not to *destroy* mens lifes, but to *save* them.[17]

Williams believed that a magistrate could be a Christian, yet he had no more right to interfere with an individual's religious life than a magistrate who was not a Christian. Although a pluralistic society was the inevitable result of religious freedom as Williams envisioned it, he did not shrink from this state of affairs but insisted that "true civility and Christianity may both flourish in a state or Kingdom, notwithstanding the permission

---

16. Ibid., 3:132.

17. Ibid., 3:132-33. In the margin Williams wrote a comment regarding the civil magistrate that echoes almost verbatim what Smyth and his congregation had written in article 85 of their confession of 1612. The same sentiment was echoed by Dr. John Clarke in the confession he penned in the Boston jail in 1651. The marginal note is as follows:

> If the Civil Magistrate be a Christian, he is bound to be like Christ in saving, not destroying mens bodies. The Civil Magistrate bound not to inflict nor to suffer any other to inflict violence, stripes, or any corporall punishment for evil against Christ.

of divers and contrary consciences, either Jew or Gentile."[18] Williams identified ·those "who persecute and who pronounce judgements of imprisonment, banishment, death as if it proceeds from Gods righteous vengeance upon the *Heretics*" as the second "Beast, the *false Prophet,* Rev. 13.13."[19] This is reminiscent of Helwys' discussion of the second beast of Revelation in his *Mistery of Iniquity.*

Dr. Cotton had argued in his *Bloudy Tenent, washed and made white in the bloud of the Lambe* that Massachusetts punished dissenters only for sinning against their own consciences. To this Williams replied, "Mr. *Cottons Distinction* of not persecuting a man for his *Conscience,* but for *sinning against* his *Conscience,* is but a *Figleafe* to hide the *nakedness* of that *bloudie Tenent.*"[20] He also argued that to persecute dissenters brings civil turmoil, not peace, and that those who persecute are more in error than any they persecute,

> [even] a *turke,* a *Jew,* a *Pagan,* an *Anti-Christian* (under the pretense that this *pagan,* this *Turke,* this *Jew,* this Anti-*Christian* sins against his owne *Conscience,*) doth not this *persecution,* I say, hould a greater *Errour,* then any of the foure, because he borders [supports] such *Conscience* in their *Errours* by such his *persecution,* and that also to the overthrowing of the *civill* and *humane Societie* of the *Nations* of the World, in point of *civill peace?*[21]

Williams' most famous metaphor in illustrating what he considered the ideal relationship of church and state is a ship at sea. By using this analogy, he attempted to dispel the notion that he was promoting anarchy by advocating religious liberty:

> There goes many a ship to sea, with many hundred souls in one ship, whose weal and woe is common, and is a true picture of a commonwealth, or a human combination or society. It hath fallen out sometimes, that both papists and Protestants, Jews and

---

18. Ibid.
19. Ibid., pp. 132-33.
20. Williams, *The Bloudy Tenent yet More Bloudy,* in *The Complete Writings of Roger Williams,* vol. 4, p. 474.
21. Ibid.

Turks, may be embarked in one ship; upon which supposal I affirm, that all the liberty of conscience that ever I pleaded for turns upon these two hinges—that none of the papists, Protestants, Jews, or Turks be forced to come to the ship's prayers or worship, or compelled from their own particular prayers or worship, if they practice any. I further add, that I never denied that, notwithstanding this liberty, the commander of this ship ought to command the ship's course, yea, and also command that justice, peace, and sobriety, be kept and practiced, both among the seamen and all the passengers. If any of the seamen refuse to perform their services, or passengers to pay their freight; if any refuse to help, in person or purse, toward the common charges or defense; if any refuse to obey the common laws and orders of the ship, concerning their common peace or preservation; if any shall mutiny and rise up against their commanders and officers; if any should preach or write that there ought to be no commanders or officers, because all are equal in Christ, therefore no masters nor officer, no laws nor orders, or corrections nor punishments;—I say, I never denied, but in such cases, whatever is pretended, the commander or commanders may judge, resist, compel, and punish such transgressors, according to their deserts and merits.[22]

There is no doubt that Williams was a profound thinker—perhaps, as he has been called, the most original thinker the American colonies produced. He considered himself a Calvinist, yet he was not in the mold of either Geneva or Dort. He was much closer to the General Baptists of England than to any other contemporary group. Accordingly, it is not surprising that the church he founded at Providence was by 1652 numbered among the General Baptist churches in the colonies. Williams was not a man of completely original ideas: he readily admitted that his ideas were anticipated by others before him, and he even used manuscripts and tracts he had discovered while in England.[23] Perhaps his greatest contribution lay in the fact that through the crucible of his own experience he was able to implement for

22. Williams, cited by Roland Bainton in *The Travail of Religious Liberty*, p. 226. Bainton has modernized the spelling.
23. Williams, *The Complete Writings of Roger Williams*, vol. 3, pp. 61-62.

the first time in history a democratic government within a state that guaranteed complete religious liberty, not mere toleration. And all of this was accomplished by a man who was profoundly committed to the Lordship of Jesus Christ. In fact, his confidence in the gospel convinced him that in a free society such as he proposed, the religious vacuum created by the absence of an established church would be filled by new converts who would embrace the faith to which he continued to give his allegiance unto death. Characteristic of this "prophet in the wilderness," as Perry Miller has called him, was his undying commitment to religious liberty, which he expressed as follows:

> Having bought truth dear, we must not sell it cheap, not the least grain of it for the whole world, no, nor for the saving of souls, though our own most precious. Least of all for the bitter sweetening of a little vanishing pleasure: for a little puff of credit and reputation from the changeable breath of uncertain sons of men. . . . Oh, how much better if it would be from the love of truth, from the love of the father of lights from whence it comes, from the love of the son of God, who is the way and the truth, to say as He (John 18:37), "For this end was I born and for this end came I into the world, that I might bear witness to the truth."[24]

DR. JOHN CLARKE CONFESSES HIS FAITH

Although not as significant in the struggle for religious freedom in England and America as Williams, John Clarke was far more important in the emergence and the shaping of the Baptist movement in the colonies than Williams was. Born in Westhrope in Suffolk County, England, in 1609, he came to Massa-

---

24. Williams, cited by Miller in *Roger Williams: His Contribution to the American Tradition*, p. 111. Miller's version is much more readable than the original, but he has lost an original emphasis, because Williams capitalized "truth" throughout these closing paragraphs of "To every Courteous Reader," the preface to *The Bloudy Tenent of Persecution*. See Williams, *The Complete Writings of Roger Williams*, vol. 3, p. 13.

chusetts Bay in 1637, at which time he found the whole colony in an uproar over the antinomian teachings of Mrs. Anne Hutchinson and her followers. Clarke was dismayed to find that the intolerance he had experienced in Old England was in the process of repeating itself in New England. Upon that occasion he wrote,

> I thought it not strange to see men differ about matters of Heaven, for I expect no less upon the earth. But to see that they were not able so to bear with others in their different undertakings and consciences as in these uttermost parts of the world to live peaceably together, whereupon I moved the latter, (Antinomians) for as much as the land was before us and wide enough with the profer of Abraham to Lot, and for peace sake, to turn aside to the right hand or to the left.[25]

His proposal for separation met with an enthusiastic response. Subsequently, he and the Hutchinson party moved to the north of Boston, but they found the winters too harsh there. Finally, with the help of Roger Williams, they were able to purchase from the Indians the island of Aquidneck, which later was given the name of Rhode Island. First a colony was formed at Portsmouth, and a short time later a second colony was established at Newport, both on the basis of civil and religious liberty.

From its beginning, Rhode Island was far larger than Providence. In addition, it apparently included a number of well-educated citizens who had experience in government. Clarke himself was a man of considerable attainments. Like Williams, he was an accomplished linguist and university trained. He had apparently studied medicine at the University of Leyden and possibly theology. At some point in his pilgrimage he had become a Separatist or even an Anabaptist. Due to the lack of adequate documentation, little is known for certain about Clarke before he arrived in Boston. By that time he was a Separatist.

In 1639 Governor Winthrop observed that the Aquidneck

---

25. Clarke, cited by Wilbur Nelson in *The Hero of Aquidneck: A Life of Dr. John Clarke* (1938; repr. Bloomfield, N.J.: Schaefer Enterprises, 1954), p. 27.

colonists had formed a church "in a very disordered way." This may have meant nothing more than that Clarke and his colleagues had refused to accept fraternal messengers from the Puritan churches of the Bay when organizing the Newport church, or that the church was suspected of harboring Baptist sentiments. In 1641 Winthrop reported that he had heard that there were Anabaptists on the island. The reports of the views on the magistracy and the sword held by Rhode Islanders could have been unfounded rumors born in the fertile imaginations of those who knew that such concepts must be present if Anabaptists were in fact on the island; however, it is probable that such views were held by some among Clarke's friends. Although it is by no means certain that the church Clarke founded at Newport was from the beginning a Baptist church, that might well be the case; if not, it is probable that it became one early on in its history. This is suggested by the involvement of a church member by the name of Mark Lukar of Greek extraction. He was numbered among the Particular Baptists in England when they began to baptize by immersion, and he became a ruling elder early in the history of the Newport church. If the church was not a Baptist church from the beginning, it is likely that it was such by 1644, when Mrs. Hutchinson, William Coddington, and others departed to form their own church. In any case, minutes of the church recorded by a Samuel Hubbard date from October 12, 1648, and they leave no doubt about the church's confessional identity.[26] Perhaps little authentic information about the church's character or about Clarke and his Baptist brethren was known in "orthodox New England" until Clarke, along with Obadiah Holmes and John Crandall, was arrested and imprisoned in Boston in 1651.

Clarke related the sad episode in his tract which was later enlarged and published in book form on May 13, 1652. Its impact was particularly significant because, despite the Westminster Assembly, England under Cromwell had taken a turn toward greater toleration of dissenters. The influence of Clarke's narrative became even more potent when Williams referred to

26. Ibid., p. 69.

the event in *The Bloudy Tenent yet More Bloudy: By Mr. Cottons endeavor to wash it white in the Bloud of the Lambe*. In this work Williams also included his letter to Governor Endicott protesting the treatment of the Baptists in the Bay. The sentiments thus aroused in England were sympathetic to the persecuted and doubtless proved effective in helping Clarke secure the charter of 1663 from Charles II.

Clarke's narrative was enlarged into a three-part book and entitled *Ill Newes from New-England*. The first part narrated the most notorious case of persecution against Baptists in New England; the second consisted of a brief confession of faith entitled "Conclusions" that Clarke wrote while he was imprisoned in Boston; and the third was a later addition in the form of a commentary on the articles of faith. Clarke's arguments for religious freedom took on a great deal more force against the backdrop of his own experience.

According to Clarke, in 1651 William Witter, an elderly blind Baptist living quietly in Lynn, two miles from Boston, had expressed a desire to have a worship service held in his home before he died. In response to his request, Clarke, accompanied by Obadiah Holmes and John Crandall, traveled on foot to Lynn. While Clarke was in the process of preaching on a Sunday morning, two constables interrupted his sermon and arrested him and his two companions. The three men were then forced to attend worship at the Congregational church. But when they refused to take off their hats as a sign of protest, they were charged with disturbing the peace and put in jail. After ten days the three were brought to trial, found guilty as charged, and fined accordingly: Clarke, twenty pounds; Holmes, thirty pounds; and Crandall, five pounds. They could choose to pay "or to be well whipt" instead. Clarke and Crandall escaped the whipping even though they refused to pay their fines, Clarke being spared when an anonymous benefactor paid the fine against his protest. But Obadiah Holmes was not so fortunate. When he too refused to pay his fine, he was given thirty lashes with a three-pronged whip. He was judged the more severely because in defiance of the law he at one time had served as pastor of a Separatist congregation at Rehoboth (which he had organized in 1649) before moving to Newport. This was not the first time a dissenter or one holding Baptist views had been publicly whipped in New England, but it was the most notorious incident, one that shocked the sensibilities of many Englishmen. Holmes' severe punishment can probably be explained by the resentment that had built up against him because he had become a Baptist. He had become a Baptist in 1649, and two years later had moved with his family to Newport. Previously he had been a faithful member of the church at Salem; in fact, two of his sons and one of his daughters had been baptized there as infants. Thus he was probably "punished" for his betrayal via the sentence he was given.

Clarke protested the sentence upon the grounds that no legal authority had been cited to support the judgment of the court. In response, Governor Endicott took it upon himself to explain the basis of the court's action:

> [Endicott] stept up, and told us we had denied Infants' baptism, and being somewhat transported broke forth, and told me I had deserved death, and said, he would not have such trash brought into their jurisdiction; moreover he said, you go up and down, and secretly insinuate into those that are weak, but you cannot maintain it before our Ministers; you may try, and discourse or dispute with them, etc.[27]

Clarke took Endicott's remarks at face value and began to prepare immediately for a forthcoming disputation. Although he was not permitted to engage in a public disputation with John Cotton or any of the other Puritan divines, the confession of faith he wrote while in prison was later incorporated in the second part of his *Ill Newes from New-England*. As such, it became an effective vehicle in giving New England a valid

27. Clarke, cited by A. H. Newman in *A History of the Baptist Churches in the United States* (New York: Christian Literature Co., 1894), pp. 136-37. See Edwin S. Gaustad, *Baptist Piety* (Grand Rapids: Wm. B. Eerdmans, 1978) for *The Last Will and Testimony of Obadiah Holmes* and • an additional biographical sketch of Holmes' life. Holmes is the most prominent figure in Clarke's narrative, which stands to reason, since for thirty years Holmes pastored the church in Newport in Clarke's absence.

account of the theological basis of the Baptist plea for religious liberty. Articles 2 and 4 reveal the depth of Clarke's conviction about the dominical nature of believer's baptism and the necessity of religious liberty:

> 2 I Testifie that Baptism, or dipping in Water, is one of the Commandments of this Lord Jesus Christ, and that a visible beleever, or Disciple of Christ Jesus (that is, one that manifesteth repentance towards God, and Faith in Jesus Christ) is the only person that is to be Baptized, or dipped with that visible Baptism, or dipping of Jesus Christ in Water, and also that visible person that is to walk in that visible order of his House, and so to wait for his coming the second time in the form of a Lord, and King with his glorious Kingdom according to promise, and for his sending down (in the time of his absence) the holy Ghost, or holy Spirit of Promise, and all this according to the last Will and Testament of that living Lord, whose Will is not to be added to, or taken from.
>
> 4 I Testifie that no such believer, or Servant of Christ Jesus hath any liberty, much less Authority, from his Lord, to smite his fellow servant, nor yet with outward force, or arme of flesh, to constrain, or restrain his Conscience, no nor yet his outward man for Conscience sake, or worship of his God, where injury is not offered to the person, name or estate of others, every man being such as shall appear before the judgment seat of Christ, and must give an account of himself to God, and therefore ought to be fully perswaded in his own mind, for what he undertakes, because he that doubteth is damned if he eat, and so also if he act, because he doth not eat or act in Faith, and what is not of Faith is Sin.[28]

There is little doubt that John Cotton was behind the intolerance to which Clarke was responding. John Spur, who was fined along with John Hazell for shaking hands with Obadiah Holmes after his ordeal, reported that Cotton had delivered a sermon just before the trial of the Baptists from Newport in which he had said that "denying infants' baptism would overthrow all; and this was a capital offense; and there-

---

28. Clarke, *Ill Newes from New-England,* as cited in *American Christianity: An Historical Interpretation with Representative Documents,* vol. 1, pp. 167-68.

fore they were soul murderers."[29] Perhaps Cotton feared that a church based upon believer's baptism would undermine the foundations of the New Israel—and in this respect he was correct, because in Clarke's confession the argument for religious freedom as well as believer's baptism was based upon the lordship of Jesus Christ and the voluntary nature of the faith response to the gospel.

The following year saw John Clarke and Roger Williams on their way to England in an effort to save Rhode Island from the self-serving designs of William Coddington. Once this was accomplished, both took advantage of the new climate of toleration to advance the cause of religious freedom through the printing press.

THE TENSIONS OF FREEDOM AND LAW
IN RHODE ISLAND

That Williams was successful in securing a charter for his beleaguered colony in 1644 was as significant as it was surprising. It was issued to Providence Plantations by the Earl of Warwick and as such provided some degree of security from the little colony's intolerant and covetous neighbors. However, with the collapse of the Commonwealth and the return of Charles II to the English throne, all the island settlements faced a precarious situation, threatened not only from without by John Cotton and the New England Standing Order but also from within.

William Coddington, onetime chief magistrate of Portsmouth and Newport, had a personal ambition to bring the island settlements under his sole authority. With this in mind, he made a trip to England, where he succeeded in having the original charter set aside and in securing from the Council of State a commission (on April 3, 1651) that named him governor of the islands of Aquidneck and "Conanicut." This commission

---

29. Cited by Newman in *A History of the Baptist Churches in the United States*, p. 138.

also took precedence over the government formed in 1647 by Providence, Warwick, Portsmouth, and Newport. Coddington's precipitous action constituted a major crisis, and the settlements commissioned Williams and Clarke to make the long trip to England in order to seek the restoration of the original charter and thus revoke Coddington's claim.

With the successful completion of the mission, Williams felt free to return to New England in 1654. Clarke remained in England, practicing medicine and working to cultivate friends in high places who might help him further Rhode Island's cause. His efforts were successful. With the help of John Milton, Sir Henry Vane, and the Earl of Clarendon, he secured the Royal Charter of 1663 from Charles II. The charter contained the principles for which Williams and Clarke had been contending for more than twenty-five years.

Although the famous words engraved on the facade of the statehouse in Rhode Island have been attributed to Charles II, it is now known that Clarke first wrote those unforgettable phrases in a petition addressed to the king in 1662. The petition itself quotes the Declaration of Breda, which Charles II composed in the Dutch Netherlands while awaiting the expected summons to the English throne in April 1660. In this famous document Charles promised to show toleration and to stop persecuting those whose expression of religious opinion did not disturb the peace. The petition is reproduced as follows in Thomas W. Bicknell's *Story of Dr. John Clarke:*

> And whereas, in their humble address, they have freely declared, that it is much on their hearts (if they may be permitted) to hold forth a lively experiment, that a most flourishing civil state may stand and best be maintained, and that among our English subjects, with a full liberty in religious concernments; and that true piety rightly grounded upon gospel principles, will give the best and greatest security to sovereignty, and will lay in the hearts of men the strongest obligations to true loyalty: now, know ye, that we, being willing to encourage the hopeful undertaking of our said loyal and loving subjects, and to secure them in the free exercise and enjoyment of all their civil and religious rights, appertaining to them, as our loving subjects; and to

preserve unto them that liberty, in the true Christian faith and worship of God, which they have sought with so much travail, and with peaceable minds, and loyal subjection to our royal progenitors and ourselves to enjoy; and because some of the people and inhabitants of the same colony cannot, in their private opinions, conform to the public exercise of religion, according to the liturgy, forms and ceremonies of the Church of England, or take or subscribe [to] the oaths and articles made and established in that behalf; and for that the same, by reason of the remote distances of those places, will (as we hope) be no breach of the unity and uniformity established in this nation: Have therefore thought fit, and do hereby publish, grant, ordain and declare, That our royal will and pleasure is, "that no person within the said colony, at any time hereafter shall be anywise molested, punished, disquieted, or called in question, for any differences in opinion in matters of religion," and do not actually disturb the civil peace of our said colony; but that all and every person and persons may, from time to time, and at all times hereafter, freely and fully have and enjoy his and their own judgments and consciences, in matters of religious concernments, throughout the tract of land hereafter mentioned, they behaving themselves peaceably and quietly, and not using this liberty to licentiousness and profaneness, nor to the civil injury or outward disturbance of others, any law, statute, or clause therein contained, or to be contained, usage or custom of this realm, to the contrary hereof, in any wise notwithstanding.[30]

At last Rhode Island and its settlements had a legal status that would protect them from Massachusetts Bay and those who would disrupt the democratic process from within. Nevertheless, dissension was still a reality. It is not surprising that inner conflict continued to plague the Rhode Island settlements, because this experiment in democratic government with its promise of religious liberty was in its initial stages. Then, too, not all the early English inhabitants were equally dedicated to the principles of religious liberty, even when they understood them.

30. Bicknell, *Story of Dr. John Clarke*, pp. 192-93. Quotation marks indicate the section lifted from the Breda Declaration. (Bicknell has modernized the spelling.)

Thus it should not come as any great surprise to learn that both political and religious factions continued to disturb the tranquility of the island throughout the seventeenth century.

Perhaps the most serious of the religious quarrels was that precipitated by the Quakers. The Quakers began to arrive in New England in 1656. The harsh reception they received in the Bay Colony drove some of them to seek a more compatible refuge in Rhode Island. Here they discovered many kindred souls among those who had accompanied John Clarke to the island, but met with outspoken criticism from Roger Williams. Although Williams confined his opposition to speaking and writing against the teachings and practices of those who preferred to be called "Friends," his criticism stung nonetheless. In his book entitled *George Fox Digg'd out of his Burrowes,* Williams' lack of appreciation for George Fox and his teachings was quite evident, as was his failure to recognize the basic concepts that the Quakers had in common with the Baptists. This work contained the fourteen propositions that Williams had intended to debate with Fox, face to face, when Fox came to Rhode Island in 1672. However, Fox left the colony before Williams arrived, and as a consequence Williams ended up debating with three Quakers of dubious ability.

Although Williams made no secret of his dislike of the Quakers, whom he viewed as sincere but mistaken, he never attempted to take legal action to block the dissemination of their views.[31] He opposed them and their teachings in the arena of free debate, but he did not lift one finger to restrain them legally or physically. Edwin Gaustad has correctly assessed the situation: "Roger Williams did not like the Quakers; he despised their theology and distrusted their motives. In all this, he was not alone. He was alone, however, in asserting that their conscience should nevertheless be left free."[32]

One result of Rhode Island's open-door policy and religious freedom was the ascendency of the Quakers. "By 1676," Gaustad

31. Carl Diemer, "A Historical Study of Roger Williams in the Light of the Quaker Controversy," Ph.D. diss., Southwestern Baptist Theological Seminary, 1972.

32. Gaustad, *A Religious History of America* (New York: Harper & Row, 1966), p. 25.

writes, "an Anglican missionary referred to the Quakers as 'the Grandees of the place,' so powerful had they become in the colony's political and economic life."[33] Another result of Rhode Island's religious freedom was that the much-persecuted Jews finally found a refuge. Sephardic Jews from Spain arrived as early as 1658 and eventually became so prosperous that in 1763 they erected the most exquisitely beautiful synagogue in America.[34]

Thus Rhode Island became the citadel of freedom in the New World. By contrast, the colony that considered itself the New Israel felt constrained to defend the faith by persecuting heretics. First Williams and then Anne Hutchinson and the antinomians felt the wrath and experienced the intolerance of the Cotton-led theocracy. Once the Bay adopted the Old World practice of punishing heresy as a crime against the state, it was only a small step from banishing dissenters to whipping Baptists, and from whipping Baptists to hanging Quakers. Thus the roll call of the persecuted in this New World Geneva would include such notables—in addition to Roger Williams and John Clarke— as Henry Dunster, the first president of Harvard College; Thomas Gould, a Congregationalist turned Baptist; Margaret Brewster and Mary Dyer, Quaker agitators; and the witches of Salem; as well as a few insane and infirm who deserved better. This chain of events in the history of Massachusetts Bay Colony illustrates the point that when the state usurps judgment that belongs only to God, convictions at variance with those of the established religion amount to criminal acts punishable by law, and persecution is the lot of the defenseless minority.

Of the conflicting visions, the infant republic was to choose that of Roger Williams and Rhode Island over that of John Cotton and Massachusetts Bay. How this came to pass is not readily apparent. In fact, the contributions of Roger Williams and John Clarke had almost been forgotten when Isaac Backus and the Warren Association took up the battle for religious freedom anew. Integral to this development and indispensable to all that was to follow was the First Great Awakening.

33. Ibid., p. 67.
34. Ibid.

--------- Chapter V ---------

New Light on an Old Issue

On March 31, 1748, the parish of Titicut, Massachusetts, levied a 500-pound tax for the purpose of completing a new meeting-house for the established Congregational Church. The tax was to be collected in equal assessments from all the property owners in the parish. At the time, Isaac Backus was pastor of a recently constituted New Light Congregational Church that had sixteen members. Naturally, Backus could see no reason why his parishioners should pay for the support of a church to which they no longer belonged. Therefore, when the tax collector called on Backus, he refused to pay the tax. Backus recalled the collector's response: "He told me if I would not pay him he would immediately carry me to jail. But just as he was going to drag me away there came in a man and called him out and paid him the money, so he was forced to let me go."[1] Other New Light members were not so fortunate. Several suffered the loss of their possessions, and one went to jail, where she was confined for thirteen months.[2]

Four years later, Isaac's mother and his brother, Samuel,

1. Backus, *Isaac Backus on Church, State, and Calvinism: Pamphlets, 1754-1739*, ed. William G. McLoughlin (Cambridge: Belknap Press, 1968), p. 7.
2. Ibid.

were carted off to jail in Norwich, Connecticut, for refusing to pay taxes for the support of Benjamin Lord, the minister of the Standing Order. Mrs. Backus' brother, Isaac Tracy, was also imprisoned for the same cause, even though he was a member of the legislature at the time. Mrs. Backus remained in jail for thirteen weeks. Afterward she wrote of the experience: "October 15th the collectors came to our house and took me away to prison about nine o'clock, on a dark, rainy night. We lay in prison thirteen weeks, and were then set at liberty, by what means I know not."[3] The unknown means of liberty was Mrs. Backus' son-in-law, who paid her church tax for her. But her son, Samuel, remained in jail another week.

This new persecuting fervor unleashed by Massachusetts and Connecticut was aroused by divisions within Congregationalism fostered by the Great Awakening, now known as the First Great Awakening, which swept across the colonies, particularly New England, from 1726 until the outbreak of the Revolutionary War. A by-product of the movement was a new surge of religious liberty, molding what was to become something of a national consensus—a consensus that Massachusetts stubbornly resisted until 1833. The First Great Awakening also transformed the traditional Calvinism of Puritan New England into an evangelical Calvinism with a fervent evangelistic thrust that transformed the despised and almost moribund Baptist minority into the most influential denomination in revolutionary America. Indispensable to this remarkable development was a man by the name of Isaac Backus.

ISAAC BACKUS, 1724-1806

Isaac Backus was born on January 9, 1724, in Norwich, Connecticut. The Backus family was the leading family of the town. Isaac's father, Samuel, traced his ancestry back to England

3. Mrs. Backus, cited by T. B. Maston in *Pioneer of Religious Liberty* (Rochester, N.Y.: American Baptist Historical Society, 1962), p. 13.

through his great grandfather, who, according to family tradition, had given the town of Norwich its name. Isaac's mother was a daughter of John Tracy, a descendant of the Winslows of Plymouth Colony. The Backus family had prospered in the New World, certain of its members having attained a high degree of prominence and wealth. Isaac's father was a farmer whose death in 1740 left his eleven children fatherless and his widow in despair. Her depression found no surcease until the influence of the Great Awakening reached Norwich.

THE IMPACT OF THE GREAT AWAKENING

Little more than a century after the founding of the first English colonies in the New World, the religious fervor that had characterized the Pilgrim fathers and the Puritans suffered a sharp decline. The divisive Half-Way Covenant, which allowed children of the unconverted to be baptized (although they could not receive communion), lowered membership requirements, which made possible the inclusion of the unconverted in the life of the Congregational churches. In 1708 a modified Presbyterian system known as the Saybrook Platform, which had been vigorously opposed by many, including Isaac Backus' grandfather, led to the loss of independence of local churches in Connecticut and the further institutionalization of Congregationalism. The Presbyterians and Dutch Reformed still went through the motions of religious practice but were spiritually at a very low ebb—or so it seemed to the Pietist Theodore Jacob Frelinghuysen and his friend Gilbert Tennent.

Frelinghuysen arrived in New York in 1720 to minister to the Dutch Reformed churches in the colonies. Soon he became pastor of four churches in the Raritan Valley of New Jersey. His earnest preaching triggered a revival: his emphasis upon the new birth and the living of a consistent Christian life evoked both criticism and conversions. In 1726 an unusually large number of individuals were converted, the effects of which were felt among the neighboring Presbyterians.

In that year Gilbert Tennent, a young Presbyterian minister, began to serve a church in New Brunswick, in the vicinity of Frelinghuysen's churches. Frelinghuysen took the young man under his personal supervision, instructing him and encouraging the members of his own churches to help raise Tennent's salary. About the same time, Gilbert's father arrived from Ireland and joined the Presbyterians. Inspired by the evangelistic spirit of his son and Frelinghuysen, the elder Tennent founded a school at Nashiminy, New Jersey, to educate promising young men for an evangelistic ministry among the Presbyterians. The graduates of Log College, as the school became known, were in the forefront of the revival that began to shake the Presbyterian churches in the Middle Colonies out of their complacency, but none of the graduates were quite as effective as Gilbert Tennent.

By 1734, a spiritual awakening of significant impact was triggered by a most unlikely pastor in one of the most unlikely places. The place was Northampton, Massachusetts, where the able Solomon Stoddard had served the church as pastor for sixty years, all the while promoting the Half-Way Covenant. His successor, Jonathan Edwards, who was studious and utterly lacking in charisma, surveyed the situation with much concern. Spiritual decadence was evident on all sides. Flagrant immorality, rationalism, and Arminianism threatened everything that Edwards held dear. In response, Edwards made adjustments in traditional Calvinism, which had become cold and lifeless. He breathed new life into the doctrines of grace, insisting upon the necessity of the new birth wrought by the Holy Spirit. He also sought to recover the earlier Congregational emphasis upon a regenerate church and insisted upon the necessity of an inner call to preach before one could assume the office of pastor. Revival—unexpected by everyone with the possible exception of Edwards and his wife, Sarah—erupted with far-reaching results. Three hundred professed conversions occurred within six months in Northampton alone, and before the revival had run its course, thousands reportedly experienced the new birth.

George Whitefield, who at only twenty-four was already a seasoned evangelist, came from England to the colonies in 1740.

It was he more than anyone else who shaped the character of the Great Awakening. Even though he was an Anglican, he soon identified with the revamped Calvinism of Edwards and refused to be limited by denominational divisions. He preached wherever he was invited, and his preaching was attended by huge throngs, particularly in Boston and Philadelphia. Before the Great Awakening was eclipsed by the rising tide of nationalism on the eve of the Revolutionary War, it had achieved some significant results. Thousands (estimates run as high as 50,000) claimed to have been converted. A common evangelical understanding of the nature of the gospel and the necessity of a personal commitment to Christ for salvation became widely accepted. Since the Holy Spirit brought conviction and conversion where the gospel was preached, established churches lost their advantage, and religious liberty was thus advanced. Many of those who opposed the Great Awakening were drawn into the Unitarian movement. Perhaps Baptists, who first stood aloof, benefited the most. Their gains in membership made them the most influential denomination in some colonies.

The Great Awakening met with protests from the very beginning, even before its excesses aroused the opposition of Charles Chauncy of First Church in Boston. The Dutch Reformed were scandalized by the preaching of Frelinghuysen and even published a 246-page book against him.[4] A division also began to occur among the Presbyterians as early as 1741. But soon the "Old Side," as the traditionalists were known, was outnumbered by the "New Side," which was able to enlist a number of effective young pastors and evangelists under its banner. Supporters of the movement were dubbed "New Lights"; opposers among the Congregationalists of the Standing Order were thus known as "Old Lights." As the New Lights began to separate from the established churches to form their own congregations, they were referred to as Separate Congregationalists or simply Separatists. However, they thought of themselves as Strict Congregationalists who were seeking to form

---

4. William Warren Sweet, *The Story of Religion in America* (New York: Harper & Row, 1950), p. 139.

churches of the regenerate, believers who owned the covenant and retained the right of calling their own pastors and conducting their own ecclesial affairs.

The Baptists present an entirely different picture. Already divided as they were into General, Regular (Calvinistic), and Seventh Day groups with subgroups, they were quite well united in their opposition to the initial stages of the Great Awakening. They reasoned that God had surely washed his hands of those who had persecuted them in both Old and New England. They simply did not trust those who held so tenaciously to their established churches. Besides, since the Act of Toleration in 1689, the Regular Baptists had pretty well reconciled themselves to their status as second-class citizens. They appreciated the fact that in Massachusetts they, along with Quakers and Anglicans, were exempt from the church tax, and they tried to ignore the fact that they were barred from attending Harvard or Yale. (Princeton, once it was founded, was only slightly less restricted.) Perhaps even a greater deterrent to Baptist participation in the Great Awakening was the fact that of the twenty-one Baptist churches in New England in 1740, only four or five were Calvinistic. All the others held that Christ died to make it possible for any person to be saved, not just the elect; these churches were generally classified, although inaccurately, as Arminian.

When George Whitefield, who had returned to England to raise funds, came back to America for one of his evangelistic tours, he reportedly said, "All my chickens have become ducks"—by which he meant that his converts had become Baptists en masse. While this may have been something of an exaggeration, it is true that the Baptists experienced phenomenal growth in New England, increasing from twenty churches in 1740 to 325 churches in 1796. Further, Baptist growth was not limited to New England or limited in its subsequent impact upon the course of a nation in the process of birth. How all of this was possible can be seen in the spiritual pilgrimage of Isaac Backus, a journey that was to take this particular pilgrim from the churches of the Standing Order to the New Lights and from the New Lights to the Separate Baptists. Of Backus' significance in the separation of church and state, William McLoughlin has written,

> Isaac Backus' GREAT CONTRIBUTION to American social and intellectual history was his vigorous exposition in theory and practice of the evangelical principles of religion and society which gradually replaced Puritanism in the latter half of the eighteenth century. In particular he was the most forceful and effective writer America produced on behalf of the pietistic or evangelical theory of separation of church and state. In this respect Backus deserves to rank with Roger Williams and Thomas Jefferson.[5]

CONVERSION AND CALL

In June 1741, a religious awakening came to Norwich and its Congregational church. Upon the invitation of the pastor, Benjamin Lord, three different evangelists, all followers of Whitefield, earnestly sought to bring the people to salvation in Christ through the effective work of the Holy Spirit. Isaac's mother, who had been converted twenty years before, found fresh assurance and relief from her depression. Isaac too was converted, but not right away. For months he had desperately sought the saving grace of God, but all his efforts seemed in vain until he was out mowing in a hayfield on August 14. About that incident he wrote, "I was enabled by divine light to see the perfect righteousness of Christ and the freeness and riches of His grace. . . . The Word of God and the promise of His grace appeared firmer than a rock. . . . My heavy burden was gone, tormenting fears were fled, and my joy was unspeakable."[6]

Although many of the parish clergy among the Congregationalists first welcomed and even invited the itinerant evangelists to promote the revival in their parishes, they soon

5. McLoughlin, in his introduction to *Isaac Backus on Church, State, and Calvinism*, p. 1.

6. From the Backus manuscript in the Isaac Backus Papers at Andover Newton Theological School, as cited in *Isaac Backus on Church, State, and Calvinism*, pp. 2-3.

changed their minds. Suspicion turned to hostility, and hostility led to legal restrictions. By 1742 the legislature passed a law that prohibited preaching by anyone in a parish without permission of the established minister, and itinerant preachers were arrested when they dared to violate the new law. These actions aroused the resentment of the New Lights. As the parish churches continued to resist any change in membership requirements to assure a church that would be regenerate in the eyes of the newly awakened, these newly converted began to withdraw to form churches of their own under the leadership of pastors of their own choosing—men whom they considered called of God and Spirit-led.

Isaac and his mother were numbered among those forming just such a Separate Congregational church at Norwich on July 16, 1746.[7] Shortly after a Separate church was organized at Bean Hill near the Backus farm, Isaac received an inner call to preach. The very next Sunday he preached to the congregation, who confirmed him in his call. He spent the next year in a wide-ranging itinerant ministry that found him preaching in Connecticut, Rhode Island, and Massachusetts. In December of 1747, he accompanied Elder Joseph Snow, a Separate preacher from Providence, to Titicut, Massachusetts, where the Congregational church had been without a pastor since the formation of the parish by the legislature in 1743. Since most of the members of the parish were New Lights, they heard the young preacher gladly and asked him to become their pastor. When Backus learned that this by law would entail being examined by ministers of the Standing Order and gaining their approval, he argued that the local church alone possessed the authority to call its pastor. The matter reached an impasse. Consequently, some of the more zealous members of the congregation took matters into their own hands and asked Backus to organize them into a Separate church,

7. For a more detailed account of Backus' New Light experience, see Stanley Grenz, *Isaac Backus: Puritan and Baptist* (Macon, Ga.: Mercer University Press, 1983), pp. 67-69. For the insights of Jonathan Edwards and Joseph Bellamy on the Great Awakening, see also *The Great Awakening*, vol. 4 of *The Works of Jonathan Edwards*, ed. C. C. Goen (New Haven: Yale University Press, 1972).

one that incorporated the disputed principles dear to the New Lights. Backus complied and organized the New Lights into a church on February 16, 1748. A few months later, on April 13, the new pastor was ordained by the church with the assistance of Separate ministers from Connecticut and Rhode Island.

The church began with only sixteen members, but that soon changed. Despite its stipulation that only those who could give an account of a conversion experience could become members, the congregation grew rapidly to three times its initial size. This growth was resented by the parish, which viewed the presence of the new church as a threat to its attempts to secure the services of a college-educated pastor. In response, the parish levied a tax of 500 pounds (the act referred to at the beginning of this chapter) for the completing of a meetinghouse for the parish church. When Backus and the members of his church refused to pay, they suffered imprisonment or confiscation of property. Such experiences drove Backus to a fresh examination of the Bible regarding church-state relations.

SEPARATES BECOME BAPTISTS

Although Baptists held themselves aloof from the Great Awakening during its early stages, before long they discovered their numbers greatly augmented by new converts, mostly from the ranks of the New Lights. This development among the Separates can be clearly traced through the experience of Isaac Backus.

The Separate Congregationalist church in Titicut, Massachusetts, was still in its infancy when in 1749 two of its more zealous members began to question the scriptural basis of infant baptism. Further, they suggested that if Titicut church members became Baptists, they would be exempt from the church tax and other forms of discrimination and persecution. Backus immediately rejected this apparent appeal to self-interest, even though the question of infant baptism still bothered him. However, Backus' own desire to reorder church life according to his understanding of the New Testament convinced him that infant baptism was a practice that had to be discontinued. Was it not the means by which the church itself had become a congregation of the mixed multitude? Once convinced of the rightness of his perspective, he was baptized by immersion on August 22, 1751.

For a while the newly baptized pastor attempted to serve his church on an open-membership and open-communion basis, but from the time of his baptism on he refused to baptize infants. After a strenuous attempt on the part of the Separates to retain both the baptized and the unbaptized in their churches, division came in 1754. Finally Backus dissolved his Separate church in Titicut and organized the First Baptist Church of Middleboro on January 16, 1756. The transition from a Separate Congregationalist church to a Separate Baptist church had been a slow and painful process, but it had been accompanied by the ever-deepening conviction that God was leading every step of the way.

Once Backus had established the church in Middleboro, Massachusetts, he sought fellowship with like-minded churches. He sought to infuse the spirit of the Separates into the older established Baptist groups. As a consequence, the Baptists of New England began to experience revival and a new spirit of unity. The modified Calvinism of Jonathan Edwards and the New Lights soon replaced the "Arminian theology" that had characterized most New England Baptists. The Warren Association—an alliance made up of Baptist churches in New England that was organized at Warren, Rhode Island, on September 8, 1767—became a much-needed vehicle through which the revitalized churches could coordinate their work and advance the cause of religious liberty. Although Backus was elected clerk at the initial meeting of the association, his church did not become a member until three years later, when he was convinced that the association intended to exercise no authority over the churches.[8]

8. See Backus, *A History of New England, with Particular Reference to the Denomination of Christians Called Baptists*, vol. 2 (Newton, Mass.:

AGENT OF THE ASSOCIATION

The chief concern of the Warren Association from its inception was the cause of religious freedom. As early as 1769, before his church joined the association, Backus was named to the Grievance Committee "to prepare petitions to the General Courts of Massachusetts and Connecticut for redress of grievances and, if necessary, to petition the King in Council."[9] Two years later, Backus was asked to become the agent of the committee and the association. During the next ten years he became both the conscience of New England Baptists on church-state issues and their most vigorous spokesman. Even after the term "agent" ceased to be used, Backus continued to draw up petitions, write, and marshal Baptist forces on behalf of the cause to which, from this point on, he devoted most of his energies.

As long as Baptists were relatively few and their churches small, they were granted exemption from church taxes levied for the support of both ministers and churches of the Standing Order. But the Great Awakening changed all of that. The New Lights who had separated from the Congregationalists became Baptists in droves. In 1784, Backus estimated the number at 40,000. In some communities these new Baptists outnumbered the Congregationalists, yet they were expected, in some cases, to pay church taxes as if they had not separated at all. Faced with so many "Anabaptists"—the term the authorities used to refer to the Baptists—the authorities severely tightened the Exemption Certificate Law, thus making so many demands annually upon the Baptists that in many cases they found it impossible to comply. Every individual requesting an exemption certificate had to garner a required number

---

Backus Historical Society, 1871), pp. 154-55. See also Maston, *Pioneer of Religious Liberty*, p. 28. In Baptist polity, the local church under the lordship of Christ recognizes no higher judicature in religious concerns. Churches "associate" in order to enjoy fellowship as well as to undertake various tasks—education for the ministry, missionary work, and the addressing of church-state issues. The association exists to serve the churches, which send "messengers" to its meetings.

9. McLoughlin, *Isaac Backus on Church, State, and Calvinism*, p. 12.

of signatures attesting to the fact that this person was a Baptist and of good character; in addition, the individual had to pay a fee of three pence sterling or four pence in paper money. Even when they managed to secure the required certificates, local authorities sometimes refused to recognize their validity. Arrests, imprisonment, fines, and confiscation of property in lieu of the church tax or exemption certificates became increasingly common.

In reaction to this unjust and dishonest state of affairs, Backus led the Warren Association in 1773 to pass a resolution encouraging member churches not to comply with the law. Backus justified this act of civil disobedience with a biblical defense. The law itself, he argued, was against the law of God, because the government had wrongly assumed the right to determine those whom it would tolerate and at what price, and those who were exempt from such regulations. Backus argued repeatedly that Christ only is Lord of the church, and that therefore the government, although ordained of God to keep the peace and protect the innocent, has no jurisdiction in religious affairs.

The most celebrated case of blatant injustice against the Baptists involved the Ashfield Baptist Church. Two-thirds of the inhabitants of Ashfield, Massachusetts, were Baptists who dutifully paid their church taxes from 1761 to 1768. According to Backus' recounting, they finally drew up a petition that was presented to the General Court asking for "relief." At first the court seemed sympathetic when it ordered "that a further collection of taxes be suspended until the town was notified." Yet, as Backus reported, in the same session of the court a law was enacted that denied the Baptists in Ashfield any exemption from ministerial taxes. In the exacting of payment, several hundred acres of their lands (ten of which belonged to the minister of the Baptist church) were sold at public auction for only a small part of their real value. According to Backus' report, after the Baptist messenger had made five or six trips of more than a hundred miles to request relief from this ruling, and had waited for long periods without success, he was at last plainly told by a number of representatives "that they had a right to make that law and to keep the Baptists under it as long as they saw fit."[10]

As Backus later reported, the confiscated property included a part of the church's cemetery. The court also issued a search warrant for the pastor's home and that of his father. His father, a godly man, was accused of passing a counterfeit dollar, a charge that later proved to be fraudulent. When the proper authorities failed to reverse this arbitrary action of the court, the Baptists gave notice that they were prepared to appeal to King George, which they eventually did when repeated appeals to colonial authorities proved fruitless. The king set aside the unjust Ashfield law, which compelled Backus to admit that the king had been more understanding of the Baptists' plight than had been the "Sons of Liberty."[11]

The Baptists were now accused of being unpatriotic, a charge long entertained by many. It is true that Backus and the Baptists did not approve of the Boston Tea Party, but once British troops had engaged the patriots at Lexington and Concord, the Baptists closed ranks with their Congregational and Presbyterian neighbors. But under Backus' leadership they kept up their battle for religious liberty as basic to all other unalienable rights. Backus did not hesitate to draw an analogy between the universally despised tea tax and the three-pence tax in sterling or four pence in paper currency charged for an exemption certificate. According to William McLoughlin, Backus later wrote that "the war was fought on two fronts by him and his brethren—against the British troops for civil liberty and against the patriot legislators for religious liberty."[12]

By 1774, Baptists were no longer looking to the English monarch for a redress of grievances. Instead, they turned to the Continental Congress—or, more correctly, to the Massachusetts delegation to the congress meeting in Philadelphia. Armed with a commission from the Warren Association to

10. Backus, *An Appeal to the Public for Religious Liberty,* in *Isaac Backus on Church, State, and Calvinism,* p. 327.

11. McLoughlin, *Isaac Backus on Church, State, and Calvinism,* p. 12.

12. Ibid., p. 13.

present a memorial to the Continental Congress, Backus enlisted the aid of James Manning, president of Rhode Island College (now Brown University), and John Gano, a Princeton graduate and pastor of the First Baptist Church of New York City. After arriving in Philadelphia, the three men were joined by a large number of Baptists and Quakers in Carpenters Hall on October 12. Manning read the memorial, after which Backus spoke to the issues raised in the document. The meeting lasted about four hours. Of those making up the Massachusetts delegation, Caleb Cushing appeared to be the most conciliatory. Robert Treat Paine refuted Backus' contention that the Baptist refusal to pay the exemption tax was a matter of conscience: "There was nothing of conscience in the matter, it was only contending about paying a little money." Samuel Adams claimed that the complaint came from the "enthusiasts" only and that "Regular" Baptists were very quiet. At the close of the long and stormy session, Backus later reported that John Adams said, "We might as well expect a change in the solar system, as to expect that they [Massachusetts] would give up their establishment."[13] Backus and his brethren were disappointed, because they had expected better from the Adams brothers, particularly Samuel. Samuel was on record as approving of Locke's treatise on toleration.

Despite suffering this kind of treatment, the Baptists were to prove themselves ardent patriots during the Revolutionary War. Only one Baptist minister, Morgan Edwards, is known to have sided with the British. Although some, such as Martin Kaufman of Virginia, refused to bear arms, a company of Baptist soldiers from Virginia fought at Valley Forge, and some pastors like John Gano served as chaplains during the war. In fact, Gano was George Washington's chaplain.

In spite of all this, when Massachusetts drew up its constitution of 1778, it still required a religious tax. Although this constitution was rejected by the towns, Article Three of the constitution of 1779 also provided for the support of an estab-

13. Cited by Joseph Martin Dawson in *Baptists and the American Republic* (Nashville: Broadman Press, 1956), p. 71.

lished church through a compulsory tax. The article did not receive the required two-thirds vote of the constitutional convention, and the Baptists carried on a year-long protest against it. Nevertheless, Article Three was allowed to remain in effect even after Backus' death in 1806.[14] Finally, in 1833, Massachusetts did give up its establishment. By this time the Congregational churches of the Standing Order had become largely Unitarian.

PRINCIPLES OF TRUTH

Although Backus never lived to see either the separation of church and state or the "sweet harmony" between the two in Massachusetts that he had advocated for so long, he well knew that these things would eventually happen. By the time of his death, two important advances had occurred: the Constitution of the infant republic had been adopted, which explicitly prohibited any religious test for public office; and the First Amendment, with its "no establishment" clause, had been ratified by the states. No doubt Backus took some satisfaction in knowing that he had had a hand in shaping the new nation, even if only indirectly. John Leland, a personal friend of Thomas Jefferson and a champion of religious liberty in Virginia, was indebted to Backus both for the inspiration he provided and to some extent for the new light he shed on the old issue of church-state relations. And Leland did live to see the collapse of the established church in both Massachusetts and Connecticut.

14. In the last tract that Backus wrote on church-and-state issues, *A Door Opened for Equal Christian Liberty* (found in *Isaac Backus on Church, State, and Calvinism*, pp. 427-38), Backus reported on the Balkam case. This case centered on Elijah Balkam, a Baptist who had complied with the law yet was subject to the religious tax. He refused to pay it because the new constitution (of 1779) had declared, "No subordination of any one sect or denomination to another, shall ever be established by law." Balkam and his lawyer also argued that "religion was prior to all states and kingdoms in the world and therefore could not in its nature be subject to human laws" (p. 432). Balkam won his case, and Backus claimed this action of the county court of Taunton effectively set aside the Standing Order—but apparently it did not.

Then too, Backus' enormous literary output was destined
to live long after his death, to inspire and inform countless
others about who the New Lights were and why they objected
so strenuously to paying a three- or four-pence tax for their
exemption certificates or a church tax for the support of the
established church. Of the forty-four books and pamphlets
Backus wrote, seven were specifically devoted to the subject of
religious liberty. From these it is possible to glean the basic
principles of Backus' thought on the subject and the context
within which he developed these principles.

Among the works Backus devoted to religious liberty and
the disestablishment of the Standing Order, the two most
important were *An Appeal to the Public for Religious Liberty*,
first published in 1773, and *Government and Liberty Described*,
published in 1778. These two works probably did more to
change public opinion on the issues at stake than any of the
other numerous petitions that Backus and the Baptists were
constantly producing. Of the latter booklet, William McLoughlin writes, "The tract was a brilliant performance, the best piece
that Backus ever wrote as a lobbyist for the Baptists. It was
weakened only by the self conscious effort of the Warren Association to assert its loyalty to the patriot cause. But even this
gave them an opportunity to indicate the rapid growth of their
denomination, which may not have been known to the general
populace."[15]

These two works were indeed "tracts for the times" that
reveal much about the sources upon which Backus drew to
support his own position. The Bible is foremost among these
sources; Backus also quoted Roger Williams and John Locke.
Although Backus referred to Locke more often, it is evident that
he was quite familiar with the tribulations of Williams and *The
Bloudy Tenent of Persecution* as well as John Clarke's *Ill Newes
from New-England*. His appreciation for Williams is transparent
in his sympathetic portrayal of the arbitrary way in which the
Bay Colony handled the Salem protest:

15. McLoughlin, *Isaac Backus on Church, State, and Calvinism*,
p. 347.

The next time their assembly met they took away a valuable tract of land from his church till they should give the court satisfaction upon these matters. For this Mr. Williams and his church wrote letters of reproof to the church where those rulers belonged, but instead of repenting of this iniquity they banished him out of their colony. Thereupon he went and found the first civil government that ever established equal religious liberty since the rise of Antichrist. And soon after [he] gathered the first Baptist church in America. He also did the most to prevent the ruin of all these colonies by the Indians of any one man in the country. Thus he overcame evil with good, while the advocates for the use of secular force in religion have requited him and his friends evil for good ever since.[16]

Although, as William McLoughlin points out, Backus quoted Locke much more extensively than he quoted Williams, he did so not, as T. B. Maston has suggested, because he agreed more with Locke but because Locke was far more palatable to New England theocrats than Williams. As McLoughlin correctly points out, Locke was primarily concerned "to protect men from civil punishment for heresy and from civil disabilities for non-conformity."[17] Locke had nothing to say against the establishment of the Church of England or the payment of taxes for its support. In fact, Backus was much closer to Williams (and Clarke) than to Locke. By 1772 Backus had begun to work toward the disestablishment of the Congregational Standing Order,[18] and it is significant that in this "third phase" of his life, to use Stanley Grenz's phrase, Backus rediscovered Roger Williams. At this point the older Baptist tradition of religious liberty, the separation of church and state, and the New Light pietism of Backus merged. As a result, in *Government and Liberty Described*, Backus began to use Locke but at the same time reinterpreted Locke to suit his purposes.

Noah Alden, a delegate to the constitutional convention called for the purpose of framing a new constitution for the state

16. Backus, *Government and Liberty Described*, in *Isaac Backus on Church, State, and Calvinism*, pp. 353-54.
17. McLoughlin, *Isaac Backus on Church, State, and Calvinism*, p. 43.
18. Grenz, *Isaac Backus: Puritan and Baptist*, p. 327.

of Massachusetts, asked Backus for his insights on the subject. This was incentive enough for Backus to compose a bill of rights that Alden might draw upon. Although the convention was not prepared to listen to a Baptist or consider a bill of rights introduced by a Baptist, the bill does give the contemporary reader some valid insights into Backus' thoughts on the role of government in religious affairs.

A basic tenet of Backus' view of government concerned its source of authority. Accordingly, Backus wrote in Article 4, "As all civil rulers derive their authority from the people, so they are accountable to them for the use they make of it." Backus spelled out the purpose of government in Article 5: "The great end of government being for the good of the governed and not the honor or profit of any particular persons or families therein, the community hath an unalienable right to reform, alter, or new form their constitution of government as that community shall judge to be most conducive to the public weal."[19]

After affirming the concept that all persons are born "equally free and independent, and have certain natural, inherent and unalienable rights," Backus proceeded to outline what he considered the most basic of these rights in Article 2:

> As God is the only worthy object of all religious worship, and nothing can be true religion but a voluntary obedience unto his revealed will, of which each rational soul has an equal right to judge for itself, every person has an inalienable right to act in all religious affairs according to the full persuasion of his own mind, where others are not injured thereby. And civil rulers are so far from having any right to empower any person or persons, to judge for others in such affairs, and to enforce their judgments with the sword that their power ought to be exerted to protect all persons and societies, within their jurisdiction from being injured or interrupted in the free enjoyment of this right, under any pretense whatsoever.[20]

19. For the complete text of the proposed *Bill of Rights for the Massachusetts Constitution of 1779*, see *Isaac Backus on Church, State, and Calvinism*, pp. 487-89.
20. Ibid.

In Article 7, Backus provided for conscientious objection to the bearing of arms: "and no man ought to be compelled to bear arms, who conscientiously scruples the lawfulness of it, if he will pay such equivalent, nor are the people bound by any laws, but such as they have in like manner assented to, for their common good." Like many other such proposals in Backus' day, Backus' bill contained articles (articles 10-13) that provided for trial by jury, freedom of speech, freedom of the press, and the right to public assembly.[21]

Backus was not primarily a political theorist. He never held public office, although he was chosen to represent Middleboro at the ratifying convention of the new national constitution, which he approved. This was the one time he acted contrary to the wishes of most Baptists, who felt that religious liberty was not sufficiently guaranteed without a corresponding bill of rights that would make such a provision unequivocal. Although Backus held that governments were necessary in order to assure freedom and peaceful co-existence under the law, his theories of the state's role in political and religious matters were derived from his understanding of the Christian faith and the nature of the church.

Backus believed that the essence of the Christian faith, the faith by which one is justified before God, was its voluntary nature. To be valid, faith must be free from any coercive power of man or government. For Backus this principle was foundational. He held that a religious tax was an attempt to coerce conformity in that which God had left free for every individual's conscience. Some critics—among them Charles Chauncy, a Unitarian and the president of Harvard; Philips Payson, the Unitarian minister who delivered the election-day sermon in May 1778; and Robert Treat Paine, a member of the Massachusetts delegation to the Continental Congress—claimed that the Baptists were simply objecting to paying a little money that was nothing but their due. In refuting them, Backus cleverly used an argument that Chauncy himself had used ten years earlier against an Anglican establishment that might possibly be "terribly oppressive":

21. Ibid.

True, Doctor, there lies the difficulty. It is not the PENCE but the power that alarms us. And since the legislature of this State passed an act no longer ago than last September to continue a tax of FOUR PENCE a year upon the Baptists in every parish where they live as an acknowledgement of the POWER that they have long assumed over us in religious affairs, which we know has often been TERRIBLY OPPRESSIVE, how can we be blamed for refusing to pay that acknowledgement; especially when it is considered that it is evident to us that God never allowed any civil state upon earth to impose religious taxes but that he declared his vengeance against those in Israel who presumed to use *force* in such affairs, 1 *Sam*, 111, 16, 34; *Micah* 111, 5, 12.[22]

Perhaps even more important in Backus' thinking was the supreme Lordship of Christ. In words reminiscent of those of John Smyth he wrote,

And when the son of God, who is the great Law-giver and King of his Church, came and blotted out the handwriting of the typical ordinances and established a better covenant or constitution of his Church upon better promises we are assured that he was *faithful in all his house, and counted worthy of more glory than Moses.* What vacancy has he then left for fallible men to supply, by making new laws to regulate and support his worship?[23]

The answer to Backus' rhetorical question was obviously "none." In order to clarify the nature of the church for his readers, Backus repeatedly contrasted the church as instituted by Christ with civil government, which he also believed to be of God. Each has different purposes and different constituencies, he pointed out, which means that the laws by which order is maintained in society and the laws by which discipline is maintained in the church are different. All of this Backus spelled out in many places, but nowhere more clearly than in the following quotation taken from his *Appeal to the Public:*

22. Backus, *Government and Liberty Described*, in *Isaac Backus on Church, State, and Calvinism*, p. 359.

23. Backus, *An Appeal to the Public*, in *Isaac Backus on Church, State, and Calvinism*, p. 313.

And it appears to us that the true difference and exact limits between ecclesiastical and civil government is this. That the church is armed with *light and truth* to pull down the strongholds of iniquity and to gain souls to Christ and into his church to be governed by his rules therein, and again to exclude such from their communion who will not be so governed, while the state is armed with the *sword* to guard the peace and the civil rights of all persons and societies and to punish those who violate the same. And where these two kinds of government, and the weapons which belong to them are well distinguished and improved according to the true nature and end of their institution, the effects are happy, and they do not at all interfere with each other. But where they have been confounded together no tongue nor pen can fully describe the mischiefs that have ensued of which the Holy Ghost gave early and plain warnings.[24]

THE BACKUS CONTRIBUTION

It is hard to overestimate the significance of Isaac Backus' contribution to the cause of religious liberty and the separation of church and state in the revolutionary era. He personified the lasting benefits of the Great Awakening for the American experience. More than any other single individual, he was also responsible for the unification of the colonial Baptist movement. By his own personal pilgrimage he illustrated how one could simultaneously be a Calvinist, a Pietist, and hold to the institutional separation of church and state. Although not as consistent as Roger Williams in his advocacy of separation, he was far ahead of John Locke. His enormous literary output was unsurpassed by that of any other colonial Baptist. However, he and the New England Baptists together did not influence the course of the new nation to the extent that John Leland and the Virginia Baptists did.[25]

24. Ibid., p. 315.
25. In *Isaac Backus: Puritan and Baptist*, Stanley Grenz credits Backus with raising afresh the issue of the relation of church and state and doing so on a higher level than did the Quakers, who simply were seeking

A part of the explanation for Backus' failure to influence a change in the religious establishment of Massachusetts in his lifetime lay in the realities of the situation.[26] John and Samuel Adams were staunch supporters of the Standing Order, and they along with many others such as Philips Payson and Charles Chauncy were both able and adamant defenders of the established church. In Virginia, on the other hand, David Thomas, John Leland, Reuben Ford, and the dissenters won the respect and support of such statesmen as James Madison, George

---

toleration as a minority religious group (p. 72). William McLoughlin wrote that *An Appeal to the Public* contains what is probably the most succinct summary of the pietistic defense of separation Backus ever wrote:

> A first and capital article in his [Christ's] doctrine is that HE IS HEAD OVER ALL THINGS TO THE CHURCH, and that she is *complete in him*, Eph. i, 21, 22; Col. ii,10. And those are to be marked as deceivers who do not thus hold THE HEAD, Col. ii, 19-23. Another article in his doctrine is that no man *can see his kingdom* nor have right to *power* therein without *regeneration*, John i, 12, 13 and iii, 3. And the first man that offered *money* as a means of obtaining *power* therein is *marked* with an internal brand of infamy, Acts viii, 19, 23. A third article is that the whole of our duty is included in love to GOD, and love to our neighbor, Matt. vii, 12 and 22; 37-40. A fourth is that the civil magistrate's power is limited to the last of these, and that his sword is to punish none but such as *work ill to their neighbors*, Rom. xiii, 1-10; 1 Pet. ii, 13-14. A fifth is that those who receive instruction and benefit from Christ's ministers, are required freely to communicate according to their ability, to their temporal support, as they will answer it to him in the great day, Luke x, 7-12; 1 Cor. ix, 4-14; Gal. vi, 6, 7. A sixth is that none should hear nor give countenance to any teachers who bring not Christ's doctrine but pervert his gospel, as they would avoid partaking in their guilt, Prov. xix, 27; Mark iv, 24; 2 John, 10, 11 [*Isaac Backus on Church, State, and Calvinism*, p. 48].

26. As for any direct influence Backus may have had upon the Massachusetts power brokers, McLoughlin points to the fact that Samuel Stillman, pastor of the Baptist church in Boston, was asked to deliver the election-day sermon before the governor and the legislature. In *Isaac Backus on Church, State, and Calvinism*, McLoughlin writes,

> Backus, foreseeing the fight which would come when a new constitutional convention met, wrote this tract to alert his brethren; the Warren Association voted to publish it. It was one of his most effective pieces of propaganda and may well have been the cause of the legislators' decision to ask a Baptist minister, Samuel Stillman, to deliver the election sermon the following year [1773]—he was the first Baptist ever to do so. Backus helped Stillman write that part of the sermon in which the Baptist position on church and state was presented in rebuttal to Payson. [p. 346]

Mason, George Nicholas, and Thomas Jefferson. Accordingly, it was the struggle for religious liberty in Virginia that had such far-reaching consequences and such a profound effect upon the nation's early years. It is this chapter in American history that constituted the heart of a revolution within the Revolution.

Chapter VI

The Virginia Experience

The transformation of Virginia, as Rhys Isaac has shown in his social history of the colony, was accomplished by a revolution within the Revolution.[1] No other English colony experienced such a remarkable transformation in its religious orientation during the revolutionary era or with such far-reaching consequences as did Virginia. W. E. Garrison ranks it as second only to the Protestant Reformation in its effect on the course of Christian history and particularly on the American experience.[2] If Garrison's opinion is more or less valid—and I believe it is—it is vital to the understanding of the uniqueness of the American republic to discover what happened in Virginia and why.

---

1. Isaac, *The Transformation of Virginia: 1740-1790* (Chapel Hill: University of North Carolina Press, 1982), pp. 272-93.
2. Garrison, "Characteristics of American Organized Religion," in *Annals of the American Academy of Political and Social Science* 256 (Mar. 1948): 17.

THE ESTABLISHED CHURCH
IN COLONIAL VIRGINIA

Virginia was the oldest English colony in the New World. Here as in no other colony, seventeenth-century English life with both its virtues and its faults was duplicated. The landed gentry lived lives of comfort and splendor at the expense of common laborers and slaves. In this stratified society there were manifest inequities but also opportunities that enabled the privileged classes to study and govern as well as to follow more frivolous pursuits. Consequently, the quality of one's life in Virginia on the eve of the Revolution depended to a considerable extent upon one's rank in a class-conscious society.

Among the elite were the clergy of the Church of England. Just as in England, the Anglican Church in Virginia enjoyed a virtual monopoly over the religious affairs of the colony. It was by law the established church. Two hundred acres of land were set aside in each parish for the use and support of the Anglican clergy. Taxes were also levied for the state church and its projects; the monies collected were used to maintain the parish churches and the College of William and Mary. Ministers could augment their salaries by charging additional fees for services rendered. Failure to attend church or to have the newborn baptized resulted in fines of varying degrees of severity. By assessing such fines the colony attempted to keep everyone in line and church revenues intact. The most serious challenge to the Anglican monopoly was the rise of the Separate Baptists.

BAPTIST BEGINNINGS, c. 1700-1769

For a hundred years after the founding of Virginia, the religious life of the colony was so closely regulated that no dissent was tolerated, and in fact few dissenters were detected. Thomas Story, a Quaker from England, reported that in 1699 the Quakers met to worship at York City in the home of "Thos. Bonger, a Preacher among the General Baptists, and it was the first meeting of our

Friends that had been held there."[3] Before this time, there is no evidence of a Baptist presence in Virginia. However, by 1715 General Baptists had organized two small congregations in the Isle of Wight County under the leadership of Robert Nordin, who had only recently arrived in Virginia from England. Taking advantage of the Act of Toleration of 1689, Nordin applied for and received a license to preach. Unfortunately, Nordin was dead by 1725, and even though his church and one or more sister churches continued under the care of a pastor by the name of Richard Jones, by 1756 the church, although General Baptist, wrote the Philadelphia Association for help. In response the association, which was made up of Regular Baptist churches (Calvinistic), sent two preachers—Morgan Edwards, pastor of First Baptist Church in Philadelphia, and John Gano, pastor of First Baptist Church in New York City—to set in order the General Baptist churches in the South. The result of the "missionary effort" of Edwards and Gano was that most of the General Baptist churches in the Southern colonies either disbanded or readily accepted the modified Calvinism of the Philadelphia Association.

The Calvinistic or Regular Baptists, as they were known, were much more self-assured and aggressive than their General Baptist brethren. However, like the General Baptists, they also sought and received permission for legally licensed meetinghouses provided by law for dissenters, meetinghouses in which properly licensed ministers were allowed to preach. Among the most notable of these was David Thomas (1732-1801). With his ministry at Mill Creek (Opekon) and Broad Run, the Regular Baptists began to make their presence felt in the Old Dominion.

Thomas was one of the few formally educated Baptist preachers on the frontier: he was a graduate of Hopewell Academy in New Jersey, and he had received an M.A. degree from Rhode Island College. Caught up in the spirit of revival that marked the Great Awakening, in 1760 he left Pennsylvania for Virginia to serve as pastor of the Mill Creek church, formerly

3. Story, cited by Garnett Ryland in *The Baptists of Virginia: 1699-1926* (Richmond: Virginia Baptist Board of Missions and Education, 1955), p. 2.

known as Opekon. Not only did Thomas draw hundreds to his services from long distances, but also a number of young men were converted under his ministry and soon began effective itinerant ministries of their own. By 1762, Thomas, along with John Marks, another Baptist minister, had organized a new church with ten members from Mill Creek. Twenty-three new converts were baptized the next day. Thomas became pastor of the newly constituted church, which took the name of Broad Run. Subsequently the Broad Run church became the center of a vigorous evangelistic ministry that by 1766 led to the formation of the Ketocton (Ketoctin) Association, which was made up of four churches with about 142 members.

Although the Regular Baptists attempted to abide by the law, their work was not without opposition. Popular prejudice manifested itself in mob violence. When Thomas was first invited to preach in Culpeper, a mob intervened, and in Stafford he was also prevented from preaching by "Ashby's gang," which, according to Garnett Ryland, "threw a live snake and a hornet's nest into the congregation."[4] When shots were fired, a riot ensued. Baptists were also accused of hatching a plot to massacre all non-Baptists when they had increased enough to achieve a numerical advantage. Thomas ably refuted this allegation and others in debate with a Presbyterian minister and in a more lasting form in a book entitled *The Virginian Baptist*, published in Baltimore in 1774.

The book makes for interesting reading because the refutation reflects the nature of the accusations against the Baptists. It also reveals the mild Calvinism of Thomas and possibly that of his converts. In the article on predestination, Thomas wrote concerning reprobates, "It is not any decree of God, but their own unbelief, that is the cause of their perdition."[5]

Thomas also rejected the charges that Baptists were unruly in their worship and that they claimed to have received special revelations above and beyond Scripture. Apparently these allegations, as Thomas suggested, arose from the behavior

4. Ryland, ibid., p. 31.
5. Thomas, cited by Ryland in ibid., p. 25.

of the Separate Baptists, who responded with great emotional fervor to the preaching of George Whitefield and James Davenport. These Separates were to evoke even greater resentment from the established clergy and the authorities than did the more subdued Regular Baptists. They were also more insistent upon their religious freedom, which they considered their God-given right. Without their presence and their vigorous evangelism, the struggle for religious freedom in Virginia and the new nation would have been a much different story.

THE SEPARATE BAPTISTS

A by-product of the Great Awakening, the first Separate Baptist church in the South was established at Sandy Creek, North Carolina. It began with Shubal Stearns and four or five families of Separate Baptists, including the family of his brother-in-law, Daniel Marshall, who moved from Tolland, Connecticut. After spending a few months in Virginia, where their message met with little response, they moved on to Sandy Creek in the fall of 1755 and organized a church with sixteen members. Here their preaching of the gospel with fervent sincerity met with a ready response. Within a few years, the church had 500 recently baptized members and had established branches in numerous frontier settlements along the wilderness trails. New converts were encouraged to exercise their gifts, and their evangelizing activity not only garnered additional converts but also raised up a number of effective lay evangelists, some of whom were eventually ordained.

This new Separate Baptist movement was not long contained in the hills of North Carolina. Virginia, South Carolina, and Georgia soon witnessed similar developments—although not without opposition. The Regulars were suspicious of the Separates, looking askance at the emotional outbursts that often attended the "New Light" meetings. Their untutored preachers and the fact that women played a prominent part in the services (praying publicly and testifying) made them suspect in the eyes of the more traditional Baptists. The Presbyterians were also highly critical of the newcomers, harshly rejecting their doctrines. Indeed, a few of the Presbyterian ministers were not above ridiculing Baptist preachers from the pulpit. However, the most violent opposition came from the colonial authorities and the established church, both members and clergy.

CONFLICT AND CHANGE

The advent of the Separates met with the most irritated response. The Regulars made an attempt to abide by the law, but these new Baptists ignored the restrictions imposed by the courts under the Act of Toleration. Instead, they practiced a far-reaching itinerant ministry, preaching wherever they received an invitation, going from house to house or barn to barn or holding forth in the open air. When they were confined to the county jails, they often drew huge crowds by preaching through the prison bars. The rougher element of the communities, led by belligerent individuals, frequently attempted to disrupt the services of the Separate Baptists and usually succeeded. Then the preachers were arrested and hauled into court and charged with "disturbing the peace." Such was the lot of Colonel Samuel Harris, the most prominent evangelist among the early Separate Baptists in Virginia.

Prior to his conversion, Harris "had held the offices of church warden, sheriff, justice of the County Court, member of the House of Burgesses, colonel of the militia of the country and commander of the fort on Mayo for protection against the Indians."[6] But once he was converted through the evangelizing of itinerant preachers Joseph and William Murphy, he relinquished all these positions in order to give himself completely to the gospel ministry. Subsequently, he became a most effective evangelist among the Separates. He began his own itinerant ministry a year after his baptism by Daniel Marshall in 1758. Although he was a charter member of the Dan River Baptist

6. Ryland, ibid., p. 38.

Church, organized by Marshall in 1760, he did not seek ordination until some years later. At that time circumstances compelled him to make the long trip into North Carolina and secure ordination at the hands of a Separate Baptist minister by the name of James Read (Reed).

When Harris left North Carolina, Read accompanied him, and the two set out on an extended evangelistic tour that was to take them through Spotsylvania, Caroline, and Goochland counties. Harris, although not formally educated for the ministry, proved himself an effective evangelist, proclaiming the gospel under the most adverse circumstances. Given how earnest and effective they were, it is not surprising that by November 1767, Harris and Read had won enough converts to establish the Upper Spotsylvania Church (with twenty-five members), the first Separate Baptist church organized north of the James River. But this new beachhead was not established without a price: it was born amid the fires of persecution—literally speaking.

LEGAL OPPRESSION AND THE DISSENTERS' RESPONSE

Lewis Craig, who became the pastor of the Upper Spotsylvania Church in 1770, was apparently the first Separate Baptist preacher arrested for "unlawful preaching" in Virginia. In 1766, shortly after his conversion, he was brought before the Spotsylvania County Court, where he defended himself admirably. In fact, John Waller, a member of the jury, was so moved and felt such great guilt that he set out on a religious quest that led to his conversion about eight months later. (Craig himself had become a Christian only the year before, when, having heard the earnest preaching of David Thomas, he experienced a profound conversion and subsequently heeded the call to preach.) Waller, who had been known to his neighbors as "Swearing Jack," now became a thoroughly committed believer. He settled his gambling debts and, following the Separate pattern, began an itinerant ministry of his own. Soon he found himself sharing a prison cell with Lewis Craig.

On June 4, 1768, Waller and four others were arrested and charged with disturbing the peace in Spotsylvania County. The prosecuting attorney claimed, "These men are great disturbers of the peace; they cannot meet a man upon the road but they must ram a text of scripture down his throat."[7] The jury sentenced the accused to jail but offered to release them if they promised not to preach in the county for a year and a day. Three of the preachers—Lewis Craig, John Waller, and James Chiles, residents of the county—refused to so promise and were sent to jail. On the way from the Fredericksburg courthouse to the jail, they sang one of Isaac Watts' hymns, "Broad is the Road that Leads to Death." They clearly aroused the sympathies of those who witnessed the spectacle, many of whom had heard of the remarkable transformations that the gospel had wrought in the lives of these young men. After spending forty-three days in jail, they were released.

The courageous conduct of the persecuted, who often preached through prison bars, evoked widespread interest and sympathy. One of those attracted to the Separates was a young schoolteacher by the name of James Ireland. Shortly after his baptism by Colonel Samuel Harris, Ireland joined Harris on a preaching mission in northern Virginia. The result of their combined efforts was the formation of still another Separate church by the name of Carter's Run.[8] Shortly afterward, Ireland began an itinerant ministry in Culpeper County. He was immediately apprehended, and he spent five months in the Culpeper county jail subjected to immeasurable hardships—but these did not prevent his preaching through the windows of his cell to huge crowds of people, some of whom were perched in trees and on rooftops. After considerable difficulty, Ireland finally secured his own release.

7. Cited by Robert Baylor Semple in *History of the Baptists in Virginia*, first published in 1810, revised and extended by G. W. Beale (Lafayette, Tenn.: Church History Research and Archives, 1976), p. 30.

8. William L. Lumpkin, *Baptist Foundations in the South* (Nashville: Broadman Press, 1961), p. 96.

The Culpeper episode represents what was occurring wherever a policy of persecution was mounted against the dissenters. "By the end of 1774," according to Garnett Ryland, "there were churches of Separates in twenty-eight of the sixty counties of Virginia, including every one in which Baptists had been imprisoned."[9] In fact, the Separate Baptists increased to the extent that the General Association, which was made up of Separate Baptist churches, many of them only recently organized, was divided into two districts. In May 1774, the Northern District consisted of twenty-four churches, reporting 1,921 members, and the Southern District included twenty-seven churches, reporting 2,033 members. The Separate Baptists were not alone in reaping a harvest from the southern wave of the First Great Awakening. The Regular Baptists also experienced great growth, as did the Presbyterians. In fact, revival fires of the Great Awakening began to burn even in some of the predominantly German-speaking communities. As a result, John Koontz was converted and baptized in Fauquier County in December 1768. He soon became a most effective evangelist, winning many German-speaking converts, including Martin Kaufman, a Mennonite. Kaufman also began to preach with some success, mainly to the German-speaking communities in the Shenandoah Valley. Koontz was beaten by mobs many times but succeeded in winning numerous converts over a forty-year period, during which time he served as pastor at Mill Creek.

Although no one died or was executed as a result of the attempt to suppress dissenters in Virginia, many were beaten at the hands of both mobs and county authorities. One of the more brutal cases involved John Waller. In the spring of 1771 he was preaching in Caroline County when he was interrupted by the parish minister, the parish clerk, and the county sheriff. While Waller attempted to pray, the sheriff ran the handle of a horsewhip down his throat; then Waller was brutally beaten. But he was undeterred, as Morgan Edwards relates. Although Waller was "bloody and disheveled" after the whipping, he continued

9. Ryland, *The Baptists of Virginia: 1699-1926*, p. 85.

his sermon. The effect was remarkable. Virtually everyone in the audience cast his or her lot with the Baptists.[10]

Legal reprisals brought unforeseen results. Widespread publicity led to a sympathetic hearing by both the masses and the elite. Not many of the landed gentry joined the dissenters, but a number of significant Anglicans began to champion the dissenters' cause. In addition, some Presbyterians who also suffered as dissenters joined the clamor for freedom. Leaders in the battle for souls and freedom were able and vigorous young men like Lewis and Elijah Craig, John Waller, and James Ireland as well as a host of others. Doubtless the reckless courage of the recent converts lent itself to a most convincing witness among their neighbors and friends. And early on the Baptist-led dissenters began to plead their cause before the House of Burgesses. As organized dissent began to speak with one voice, petitions became an increasingly potent tool.

PETITIONS, 1768-1776

By 1770, Baptists had begun to petition the House of Burgesses for relief from the perverse interpretations of the Act of Toleration that had led to widespread oppression. As early as 1768, however, the Separates petitioned county authorities for licenses for both ministers and meetinghouses—although usually without success. For example, on October 27, 1768, thirty-two citizens in Amelia County made this request of the court: "We the subscribers do humbly pray that your worships would favor us so far as to license George Walton's house as a place for those dissenters called Separate Baptists to assemble and preach in. Therefore [we] humbly submit the consideration to your worships, hoping you will in mercy grant the same, to us who are in duty bound to always pray for all authorities under God and

10. Edwards, cited by Lumpkin in *Baptist Foundations in the South*, p. 98.

over us."[11] On the back side of the petition the court later recorded these words: "Dissenters petition called Baptist. Rejected. 14th Nov. 1768."

The first petition addressed to the House of Burgesses fared no better than earlier petitions addressed to local authorities. This first petition contained two requests. First, the petitioners asked that their preachers be excused from attending muster in discharging their military duty, a request that was denied. Second, they asked that Baptist meetings not be limited to licensed meetinghouses, a request that was not acted upon. However, the petitioners would not be so easily turned aside.

In 1772, petitions were forthcoming from a number of counties in which dissenters had met with a policy of legal oppression. One petition asked the House of Burgesses that Baptists "be treated with the same indulgence, in religious matters, as Quakers, Presbyterians and other Protestant dissenters enjoy."[12]

A petition from Amelia County Baptists, addressed to the House of Burgesses and dated March 14, 1772, asked for "liberty of conscience" in addition to a redress of grievances. The petition indicates that Baptists were aware of the popular prejudice against them and in response assured the authorities of the nonpolitical nature of their movement:

> [If] the Power of granting Licenses to Teachers, be lodged, as is supposed, in the General Court alone, the Petitioners must suffer considerable inconveniences, not only because that court sits not oftener than twice in the Year, and then at a Place far remote, but because the said Court will admit a single Meeting-House and no more in one County; and that the Petitioners are loyal and quiet Subjects, whose Tenets in no wise affect the State; and, therefore praying a Redress of their Grievances, and that Liberty of Conscience may be secured to them.[13]

11. A photostatic copy of this petition is reproduced in Lewis Peyton Little's *Imprisoned Preachers and Religious Liberty in Virginia* (Lynchburg, Va.: J. P. Bell Co., Inc., 1938), p. 146.
12. Cited by Ryland in *The Baptists of Virginia: 1699-1926*, p. 92.
13. Ibid., p. 93.

On May 17, a bill for extending the Act of Toleration to Protestant subjects "dissenting from the Church of England" was reported out of committee. This bill was even more restrictive than previous measures regulating dissenters. Although it never came to a vote, the news of its strictures on non-Anglican worship in the colony elicited a rash of new petitions from Separate Baptists, Regular Baptists of the Ketocton Association, and the Presbytery of Hanover "on behalf of themselves and all Protestant dissenters in general."[14]

Up until August of 1775, the Baptist and Presbyterian petitioners had simply protested against the laws regulating dissenters. Now the impending Revolutionary War presented a new opportunity for dissenters. Freedom was in the air, and they intended to make the most of it. Anticipating independence from England, the House of Burgesses of Virginia called for the convening of a convention to make the transition from colony to state. This constituted a signal for the Separates to act. The Northern and Southern Districts of the Separate Baptist General Association met in August 1775 in Du Puy's meetinghouse (named for John Du Puy, a former pastor), where the delegates decided to circulate petitions throughout the state addressed to the Virginia Convention asking "that the church establishment should be abolished, and religion left to stand upon its own merits, and [that] all religious societies should be protected in the peaceable enjoyment of their own religious principles and modes of worship."[15] According to Garnett Ryland, this was "the first organized action" taken in Virginia calling for religious freedom and the separation of church and state.[16]

In a separate action, the General Association addressed a petition to the convention (which was in session at the time) affirming their support of "a Military resistance against Great Britain." They also asked that they have "free Liberty to preach to the Troops at convenient times without molestation or

14. Ibid., p. 95.
15. Cited by Semple in *History of the Baptists in Virginia,* p. 85.
16. Ryland, *The Baptists of Virginia: 1699-1926,* p. 95.

abuse."[17] Four ministers—Elijah Craig, Lewis Craig, Jeremiah Walker, and John Williams—were chosen to hand-deliver this petition to the convention, which was meeting in Richmond. Significantly, three of these four men had been among the first to be legally arrested and imprisoned in Virginia. The petition they presented met with a favorable response. The delegates to the convention were greatly encouraged by this indication of support and promptly passed a resolution permitting dissenting clergymen to "celebrate divine worship, and to preach to the soldiers, or to exhort from time to time, as various operations of the military service may permit."[18] (Before the war was over, even George Washington had as chaplain a dissenting clergyman named John Gano.) Although few if any realized it at the time, this action signaled the beginning of the end of the established church in Virginia.

Thus the Baptists joined the Revolution with other patriots but for fundamentally different reasons. Their major concern was religious liberty, which had been denied them. They overcame their reluctance to bear arms for the sake of identifying with the Revolutionary cause. Less than five years before, the venerable old preacher Shubal Stearns had, in the midst of the Regulator uprising in North Carolina (which was crushed in the "War of Regulation" in 1771), led the Sandy Creek Church to pass a resolution excluding any member who would take up arms.[19] Despite their reluctance to bear arms in the Revolution, the dissenters saw a way to significantly further their own revolution, the cause of religious freedom. Accordingly, virtually all attempts by Stearns and his fellow Baptists to follow the course of nonviolence were to fail. Only a few Baptists under

17. In *The Baptists of Virginia: 1699-1926* (p. 96), Ryland reproduces the petition in its entirety; the original is found in the Virginia State Library.

18. Ibid., p. 97. This positive response was the first breakthrough in the stalemate that existed between the Baptists and the authorities in Virginia.

19. The Regulator movement began in 1758 as a protest against unjust taxes by the government. It was greatly exacerbated when William Tryon, a fanatical Anglican, became governor. It was public knowledge that he was an unjust ruler who hated the Baptists. He used the Regulator movement as an excuse to harass and persecute them.

the influence of Martin Kaufman, a former Mennonite, persisted in holding to nonresistance.

The Separate Baptists' expression of support for the patriots effectively scotched the rumors of anarchy that were constantly circulated by their enemies. Furthermore, for the first time they received a favorable hearing from Virginia lawmakers. James Madison, who had almost despaired of ever seeing an end to the official persecution of dissenters in Virginia, took heart. Only the year before, on April 1, 1774, he had written William Bradford, Jr., in Philadelphia, expressing his doubts concerning greater toleration of dissenters:

> Petitions, I hear, are already forming among the persecuted Baptists, and I fancy it is in the thought of the Presbyterians also to intercede for greater liberty in matters of religion. For my own part, I cannot help being very doubtful of their succeeding in the attempt. The affair was on the carpet during the last session; but such incredible and extravagant stories were told in the House of the monstrous effects of the enthusiasm prevalent among the sectaries, and so greedily swallowed by their enemies, that I believe they lost footing by it. And the bad name they still have with those who pretend too much contempt to examine into their principles and conduct, and are too much devoted to ecclesiastical establishment to hear of the toleration of dissentients, I am apprehensive, will be again made a pretext for rejecting their requests.[20]

In two years the climate had changed to the extent that on May 15, 1776, the Virginia Convention instructed its delegates to the general conference in Philadelphia to prepare a declaration of independence, which they did. Next the convention proceeded to adopt a bill of rights. It is evident that the dissenters had made their point, for the sixteenth article called for "the fullest toleration in the exercise of religion, according to the dictates of conscience, unpunished and unrestrained by the magistrate." In response to a motion by James Madison, the word "toleration" was stricken and the article reworded to read as follows:

20. Madison, cited by Ryland in *The Baptists of Virginia: 1699-1926*, p. 94.

That religion, or the duty which we owe our creator, and the manner of discharging it, can be directed only by reason and conviction, not by force or violence and, therefore, all men are equally entitled to the free exercise of religion according to the dictates of conscience; and that it is the mutual duty of all to practice Christian forbearance, love and charity towards each other.[21]

By this time the Baptists could no longer be quietly ignored. Not only had their rapid growth—in spite of popular prejudice and legal reprisals—caught the attention of the statesmen, but also the Presbyterians of the Hanover Presbytery and other dissenters now joined them in circulating a petition that secured almost ten thousand signatures. The General Association drew up the petition in August 1775 and circulated it throughout the state. William Fristoe describes the effort to secure as many signatures as possible:

> That we might the better be prepared to address the state legislature, petitions were circulated in every direction to the extremities of the state. The Presbyterians concurred with us, for they had in some respects been like sufferers, and numbers of the Episcopalians had become sensible of the injustice with which we had been treated, and afforded their aid by signing our petition, so that when our address was presented in the House of the Assembly, the number of signers was found about 10,000, and for the first time obtained a successful hearing. By act of Assembly establishment of religion, in part, was abolished so far as it respected compulsory measures to pay the parson's salary, and secured to every denomination the right of worshipping God according to the dictates of their own conscience, and that no person was to suffer in his person or property on account of his religious tenets, nor be prevented in the free exercise of them.[22]

21. Cited by Ryland in ibid., pp. 97-98.
22. Fristoe, cited by Ryland in ibid., p. 101. From 1772 to 1774, the petitions of the Baptists took on a different tone. In February and March of 1772 petitions requesting the same privileges as "Quakers, Presbyterians, and other Protestant dissenters" were sent to the House of Burgesses from Mecklenburg, Sussex, and Caroline counties. But "towards the close of the year 1774," wrote Robert Baylor Semple, "they [Baptists] began to entertain

Taking advantage of the new climate of toleration, the framers of the petition underscored the cry for freedom of religion:

> Your Petitioners therefore having long groaned under the Burden of an Ecclesiastical Establishment beg leave to move your Honourable House that this as well as every other Yoke may be broken and that the oppressed may go free: that so every religious Denomination being on a Level, Animosities may cease, and that Christian Forbearance, Love and Charity, may be practised towards each other, while the Legislature interferes only to support them in their just Rights and equal privileges.[23]

With this petition the floodgates were opened. Petitions now began to pour in from all sides. The Presbyterians, who had suffered many of the same deprivations and hardships as the Baptists but who had, up until 1776, sought relief only under the Act of Toleration, were now thoroughly aroused.

Caleb Wallace, a member of the Hanover Presbytery who recognized that the assembly had no intention of disestablishing the Episcopal Church, wrote, "It is manifest that our Assembly designed to continue the old Church Establishment. The Baptists circulated a Counter Petition signed by above 10,000 Freeholders."[24] These "freeholders" included, in addition to the Baptists, both Presbyterians and even a few Episcopalians who also sought the disestablishment of the Episcopal Church as well as religious freedom.

Other dissenters reacted in different ways. The Lutherans sought relief too, but only from taxation to support the established church, at the same time assuring the legislature that they were "not breaking from the established church as do the Common Discenders."[25] Understandably, Methodists, who still considered themselves a part of the Episcopal Church,

---

serious hopes, not only of obtaining liberty of conscience, but of actually overturning the Church Establishment" (Semple, *History of the Baptists in Virginia*, p. 43).

23. Cited by Ryland in *The Baptists of Virginia: 1699-1926*, pp. 99-100. The original petition is in the Virginia State Library.

24. Wallace, cited by Ryland in ibid., p. 100.

25. Cited by Ryland in ibid., p. 102. The original petition is in the Virginia State Library.

continued to support the establishment until 1784. The Mennonites and the Quakers remained "the quiet in the land" while supporting the cause of religious freedom.

Although the implications of the Virginia Declaration of Rights of 1776 were generally ignored, at least dissenters could no longer be legally considered criminals. In a sense the battle for the disestablishment of the Episcopal Church and the establishment of complete religious liberty in Virginia had just begun. In their struggle for freedom, the dissenters were now joined by able preachers and the most brilliant and politically astute statesmen of the Revolutionary era.

THE CRUCIAL DECADE: 1776-1786

Edwin Gaustad is surely correct when he writes, "The half century between the Declaration of Independence in 1776 and the deaths of Thomas Jefferson and John Adams in 1826 were years of momentous option and crucial decision."[26] Of this period, the crucial decade was the first. During this ten-year period an informal coalition was formed between rationalists (Deists) and dissenters that in time would lead not only to the establishment of religious liberty and the disestablishment of the Episcopal Church in Virginia, but also, in 1789, to the First Amendment to the Constitution.

Up until 1784, the barrage of petitions coming from the beleaguered Baptists had led to little more than the decriminalization of religious dissent. The dissenters had won few advocates in the House of Burgesses, most of its delegates considering the miscellaneous collection of dissenters a nuisance at best—that is, until James Madison became a delegate to the Virginia Convention. The convention had been called to form a transitional government to help Virginia move from colony to state. After instructing the Virginia delegation to the Continen-

26. Gaustad, *Faith of Our Fathers: Religion and the New Nation* (San Francisco: Harper & Row, 1987), p. 1.

tal Congress to make the motion separating the English colonies from the mother country, the convention turned its attention to composing a declaration of rights and a constitution.

George Mason, a member of the Committee on Privileges and Elections who was known as the "apostle of civil liberty," was charged by the committee with the responsibility of drafting the declaration of rights, which was published in the *Virginia Gazette* on June 1, 1776. The declaration consisted of an introductory paragraph and sixteen articles spelling out the implications of freedom and equality in the new state. Article XVI dealt with religion "and the manner of discharging it," which, the article went on to declare, "can be governed only by reason and conviction, not by force or violence; and therefore . . . all men should enjoy the fullest toleration in the exercise of religion, according to the dictates of conscience."[27] The words as well as the sentiment expressed were but an echo of the petitions offered by dissenters, with the exception of the concept of toleration, which they were no longer willing to accept. Neither was young Madison, who had been added to the committee. He offered an amendment that significantly altered the article: "[that] all men are equally entitled to the free exercise of religion and therefore that no men or class of men ought on account of religion to be invested with peculiar emoluments or privileges; nor subjected to any penalties or liabilities."[28] Madison even persuaded Patrick Henry to present the amendment, but when it became evident that the whole article would fail unless the part relating to "emoluments and privileges" was deleted, this amendment was stricken. Nevertheless, a blow had been struck for religious freedom. For the first time, the Commonwealth affirmed by law the individual's right to religious freedom.[29]

Although Thomas Jefferson was absent from Virginia at

27. Cited by Reuben Edward Alley in *A History of Baptists in Virginia* (Richmond: Virginia Baptist General Board, 1973), p. 98.

28. See Thomas E. Buckley, *Church and State in Revolutionary Virginia: 1776-1787* (Charlottesville, Va.: University Press of Virginia, 1977), pp. 16-19.

29. Alley, *A History of Baptists in Virginia*, p. 98.

the time because he was attending the Continental Congress, he prepared three drafts of a constitution for Virginia. The last arrived in June, too late to be given due consideration by the convention. Doubtless his statement on religion in the section entitled "Rights Public and Private" would have suffered the fate of Madison's proposal on disestablishment, because Jefferson proposed that "all persons shall have full and free liberty of religious opinion; nor shall any be compelled to frequent or maintain any religious institutions."[30]

Even though it appears that both Madison and Jefferson were quite prepared to disestablish the Episcopal Church, the majority of the delegates were not. Both Jefferson's position and that of the convention were put in historical context by Jefferson himself in his *Notes on Virginia*, which he wrote some years later. After estimating that "two-thirds of the people [in Virginia] had become dissenters at the commencement of the present revolution," he reported,

> The convention of May 1776, in their declaration of rights, declared it to be a truth, and a natural right, that the exercise of religion should be free; but when they proceeded to form on that declaration the ordinance of government, instead of taking up every principle declared in the bill of rights, and guarding it by legislative sanction, they passed over that which asserted our religious rights leaving them as they found them. The same convention, however, when they met a member of the general assembly in October, 1776, repealed all *acts of parliament* which had rendered criminal the maintaining of any opinions in matters of religion, the forbearing to repair to church, and the exercising of any mode of worship; and suspended the laws giving salaries to the clergy, which suspension was made perpetual in October, 1779.[31]

The year 1779 was indeed pivotal in the ongoing battle for religious freedom. It was in that year that Jefferson's bill for the

---

30. Buckley, *Church and State in Revolutionary Virginia: 1776-1787*, p. 20.

31. Jefferson, *Notes on Virginia*, in *The Writings of Thomas Jefferson*, vol. 2, ed. Albert Ellery Bergh (Washington: Thomas Jefferson Memorial Association of the United States, 1905), p. 219.

establishment of religious freedom was introduced into the General Assembly, which had succeeded the House of Burgesses as the governing body of the state of Virginia. The General Association of Separate Baptists, which had petitioned the House of Delegates the previous year, asking that marriages performed by "dissenting ministers" be recognized as valid, hurriedly passed a resolution commending the bill. The association promptly sent a report of their action to the *Virginia Gazette*. It read, "That the said bill, in our opinion, puts religious freedom upon its proper basis; prescribes the just limits of the power of the state, with regard to religion; and properly guards against partiality towards any religious denomination; we therefore, heartily approve of the same and wish it to pass into law."[32]

Yet, despite the growing strength of the dissenters, the bill did not survive the legislative session. It received two readings but not the required third. Instead, the House of Delegates voted to postpone further consideration until August 1. The delay was due to two principal factors. First of all, the house lacked strong leadership on the side of religious freedom because Madison was serving in the Continental Congress and Jefferson was serving as governor and thus had no effective voice in the legislative process. Second, the supporters of the established church were not inactive. Following the example of the dissenters, Episcopalians (including Methodists) had presented a number of petitions in support of the established church. The Presbyterians of the Hanover Presbytery, who had issued a well-formulated petition in support of Article XVI in the Declaration of Rights, were now conspicuous in their silence. Although Jefferson sent a copy of the bill to John Todd, one of their leading ministers, and Todd privately indicated his agreement with Jefferson, neither Todd nor any of his fellow ministers took a public stand favoring the bill. Obviously, the Presbyterians were divided. It could have been, as Thomas Buckley suggests, that the idea of levying a general assessment upon the citizenry as a whole, an assessment that would be divided proportionately

32. Cited by Ryland in *The Baptists of Virginia: 1699-1926*, p. 105.

among the various denominations, had already begun to receive favorable attention among them.[33] At any rate, the Baptists appeared to stand almost alone in their public support of Jefferson's bill. It not only failed to receive the necessary third reading; in October it was completely bypassed.

Jefferson's bill did thoroughly alarm supporters of the established church. When the assembly reconvened in October, a committee was appointed to prepare a bill "concerning religion." The committee dutifully presented such a bill, in which the influence of the Anglicans was clearly evident. It proposed to establish Christianity as "the religion of the commonwealth"; denominations would be approved if they accepted five articles of faith drawn up by the committee.[34] Because they could not subscribe to the required articles, Jews, Catholics, and Quakers were excluded and therefore not to be tolerated. Mennonites and many Baptists would also have been excluded, because the bill required ministers to take an oath in order that "the state may have Security for the due discharge of the Pastoral Office."[35] The bill also provided for "incorporation" of those approved denominations and financial support for them through taxation. After a second reading, this bill also met the fate of Jefferson's bill. It was tabled on November 15, exactly a month after it was first presented. Nevertheless, two aspects of the bill—incorporation and a general assessment—were to surface again to compel the General Assembly and the people

33. Buckley, *Church and State in Revolutionary Virginia: 1776-1787*, pp. 52-55.

34. Cited by Buckley in ibid., p. 57. The five articles were as follows:

First, That there is one Eternal God and a future State of Rewards and punishments.

Secondly, That God is publickly to be Worshiped.

Thirdly, That the Christian Religion is the true Religion.

Fourthly, That the Holy Scriptures of the old and new Testament are of divine inspiration, and are the only rule of Faith.

Fifthly, That it is the duty of every Man, when thereunto called by those who Govern, to bear Witness to truth.

35. Ibid., p. 58.

of Virginia to make some hard choices regarding the relationship of religion and government in their state.

The Role of James Madison

After an absence of four years, Madison returned from the Continental Congress in 1784 to serve once again as a delegate from Orange County in the House of Delegates. During his absence, George Mason had been able to rally the anti-establishment forces to defeat the "bill concerning religion," which sought to establish Christianity as the religion of the state. The assembly also had repealed a law of 1748 that made obligatory tax support of the Anglican clergy, although the law had not been enforced since 1776. Despite these changes, there were strong advocates, particularly in the senate, of both an incorporation bill and a general assessment bill. These advocates were led by the popular Patrick Henry.

Madison was no match for Henry's eloquence. However, he was more than Henry's match in both conviction and mental ability. Besides, as events were soon to reveal, he had the dissenters on his side, and by 1785 the dissenters constituted the overwhelming majority of church members in Virginia. Their ranks had been greatly augmented by the separation of the Methodists from the Church of England in 1784. Previously, the Methodists had supported a continuation of the Episcopal establishment, but by 1785, that support was by no means assured. Although the Presbyterians, like the Baptists, had petitioned the assembly for a change in the marriage and vestry laws, at first they had supported a general assessment bill, much to Madison's disappointment. Finally, however, they too cast their lot with the Baptists against the bill, which led to its ultimate defeat. But victory was not all that apparent in 1784.

After a number of years during which staunch Episcopalians had sought both an incorporation bill and a general assessment bill, Thomas Matthews presented on behalf of a committee for religion a resolution stating that "the people of the Commonwealth, according to their respectful abilities, ought to pay a moderate tax or contribution, annually, for the support of the christian religion, or of some christian church, denomination or communion of christians, or of some form of christian worship."[36] A committee of ten, with Patrick Henry as chairman, was appointed to draw up a bill based on this resolution. It was a foregone conclusion that the Episcopalians in the assembly would support such a bill, but when the Presbyterians presented a memorial to the assembly strongly approving the bill, provided it contained guarantees regarding their own freedom, the pro-assessment forces were elated, and Madison was exasperated. Reflecting upon the situation, he wrote during the following April that the Presbyterians were "as ready to set up an establishment which is to take them in as they were to pull down that which shut them out."[37]

However, Madison's caustic remark was not applicable to all Presbyterians or even to all ministers of the Hanover Presbytery. From the earliest stages of the discussions of bills regarding incorporation and a general assessment, William Graham, president of Liberty Hall College, had opposed both. Once the incorporation bill had passed the House of Delegates, reportedly with Presbyterian backing, the Graham-led forces sent a number of petitions protesting both incorporation and a general assessment. However, from Prince Edward County came a letter from eighty "most respectable citizens" in support of assessment, a letter that was probably inspired if not written by John Smith, a most ardent advocate of assessment among the Presbyterian clergy. Although the Presbyterians were divided over the issues of incorporation and assessment, the Hanover Presbytery supported both in their memorial, apparently presenting a solid front. Doubtless there were some ministers and some laymen among them who had serious reservations about this action of the majority.

In October 1784 the Baptists who had been presenting petitions to the legislative body of Virginia for about sixteen years set up a new structure for the express purpose of making

36. Cited by Buckley in ibid., p. 92.
37. Madison, cited by Buckley in ibid., p. 96.

a more effective lobbying effort on behalf of dissenters. Some of the more prominent ministers among them believed that a general committee composed of four delegates from each of the four associations, including the Ketocton (the association of Regular Baptists), could act more quickly and more effectively than the separate associations. William Webber was chosen moderator and Reuben Ford was elected clerk. Thus for the first time the Separate and the Regular Baptists were poised to make a concerted effort to secure complete religious liberty in Virginia. But the committee's interests and influence were to reach far beyond the bounds of the state.

In its first action, the committee sent a memorial to the General Assembly dated October 9, 1784, in which it reminded the delegates of the inequities that still existed regarding the vestry and the marriage laws. The committee also expressed the fervent desire that "every grievous Yoke be broken, and that the oppressed go free; and that in every Act the bright beams of equal Liberty and Impartial Justice may shine."[38]

At the second meeting of the committee in August 1785, Reuben Ford, clerk of the committee, gave a mixed report. He reported that at last the long-standing grievances of dissenters concerning the vestry and the marriage laws had been heard, and that the necessary amendments which put all ministers on an equal footing before the law had been passed. But he also relayed the information that a general assessment bill "establishing a provision for teachers of the Christian religion"[39] had almost become law; a final hearing had been postponed until the next session in order to give the people an opportunity to express their wishes regarding the measure. The postponement was not unprecedented, but in this case it represented the political strategy of James Madison, of which the General Committee was doubtless aware.

Madison had acquiesced to the incorporation bill because it ostensibly applied to all denominations, although everyone knew that it was designed for the benefit of the Episcopal

38. Cited by Ryland in *The Baptists of Virginia: 1699-1926*, p. 123.
39. Ibid., p. 124.

Church. However, the delegate from Orange refused to begin a battle over an issue of such dubious merit. But Patrick Henry's "Bill for Establishing Provision for Teachers of the Christian Religion" was a far different matter. Against this bill Madison would wage war at any cost. Just before the vote had been taken on the incorporation bill, Patrick Henry had been elected governor of the state, succeeding Benjamin Harrison. Given the overwhelming vote in favor of the incorporation bill in the House of Delegates, Henry probably felt assured of the successful passage of a general assessment bill even without his presence or participation in the legislature. This is how things appeared in December 1784—but appearances were deceiving.

Madison was, on the basis of principle, unalterably opposed to an assessment bill. Basically, Madison was a rationalist, but he did not hesitate to use other arguments as well. He apparently invoked John Locke but clearly went well beyond him in championing a position long held by the Baptists. In a long speech before the House of Delegates, Madison voiced the arguments that would find a more polished form in his *Memorial and Remonstrance*. Although Madison's speech doubtless had an effect, the assessment bill survived a second reading, although by a narrow margin of two votes (44 to 42). The alliance of Episcopalians and Presbyterians managed to push the bill through despite the Madison-led forces of rationalists and dissenters, including a few Presbyterians. But Madison didn't give up the fight: he knew that the strength of the dissenters was not in the General Assembly but among the common people. A motion was made to delay a third and final reading of the bill until the next session, and it passed by a vote of 45 to 38. It was suggested that this period of time would give the people an opportunity to register their support of or opposition to the bill. In order to facilitate this procedure, a motion was passed authorizing each delegate to receive twelve copies of the bill to circulate in his county.

Almost immediately, opposition to the assessment bill arose, taking many forms. Numerous articles appeared in the *Virginia Gazette* arguing against tax support for and/or government intervention in religious concerns. Seventy delegates of the 1784 assembly, twenty-one of whom had supported the incorporation and assessment bills, were not returned to office in the elections of April 1785. No doubt the anti-assessment dissenters were making their presence felt. This was clearly the case with James Pendleton of Culpeper County, long a member of the General Assembly and a leader of the pro-assessment forces. He was defeated specifically because of his support for the assessment bill.[40]

The Baptists, who made up the largest body of dissenters in the state, had begun to oppose the assessment bill in 1784. Petitions against the assessment bill were circulated in Rockingham by Silas Hart in 1784 and in Caroline by John Young in 1785. In August 1785 the General Committee resolved the following:

> That it be recommended to those counties, which have not yet prepared petitions to be presented to the General Assembly against the engrossed bill for a general assessment for the support of the teachers of the Christian Religion, to proceed thereon as soon as possible. That it is believed to be repugnant to the spirit of the gospel for the legislature thus to proceed in matters of religion; that the holy author of our religion needs no such compulsive measures for the promotion of his cause; that the gospel wants not the feeble arm of man for its support; that it has made and will again through divine power make its way against all opposition; and that should the legislature assume the right of taxing the people for the support of the gospel it will be destructive to religious liberty.[41]

Although it was evident after the elections of April 1785 that the anti-assessment forces commanded a majority of the new legislators, some of Madison's allies felt that he should make his views known through the press. Among these were Colonel Wilson Carey Nicholas of Albemarle County and his brother, George. The Nicholases, like Madison and Jefferson, were rationalists and

40. For a discussion of the role of the assessment issue in the election of April 1785, see Buckley, *Church and State in Revolutionary Virginia: 1776-1787*, pp. 116-17.
41. Cited by Ryland in *The Baptists of Virginia: 1699-1926*, pp. 124-25.

determined foes of the assessment bill. Finally, Madison was persuaded to put his own opposition to the assessment bill in print. The result was *A Memorial and Remonstrance*, his finest treatise on religious liberty, addressed "To the Honorable the General Assembly of the Commonwealth of Virginia." Nowhere else in Madison's published works is his position on religious liberty and the relation of the church and state more clearly stated.

He presented the major premise of his argument in the first paragraph:

> 1. Because we hold it for a fundamental and undeniable truth, "that Religion or the duty which we owe to our Creator and the manner of discharging it, can be directed only by reason and conviction, not by force or violence." The Religion then of every man must be left to the conviction and conscience of every man and it is the right of every man to exercise it as these may dictate. This right is in its nature an unalienable right.[42]

Further on in the same paragraph, Madison removed religion from the purview of government: "We maintain therefore that in matters of Religion, no man's right is abridged by the institution of Civil Society and that Religion is wholly exempt from its cognizance."

In the third paragraph, Madison alluded to the arguments advanced by Isaac Backus, arguments with which he was doubtless familiar because of his tenure in the Continental Congress. He appealed to reason when he wrote,

> Who does not see that the same authority which can establish Christianity, in exclusion of all other Religions, may establish with the same ease any particular sect of Christians, in exclusion of all other Sects? that the same authority which can force a citizen to contribute three pence only of his property for the support of any one establishment, may force him to conform to any other establishment in all cases whatsoever?

In the fourth paragraph, Madison presented what was basically a religious argument when he wrote that to interfere with

---

42. For the complete text of this treatise, see the Appendix.

religious freedom "is an offense against God, not against man. To God, therefore, not to man, must an account of it be rendered." Rhetorically he asked, "Are the Quakers and Menonists the only sects who think a compulsive support of their Religions unnecessary and unwarrantable? Can their piety alone be entrusted with the care of public worship?" By using small but well-known pacifist denominations as models for established religion to follow, he hoped to impress upon his adversaries the unpalatable nature of their presuppositions.

In the fifth paragraph Madison claimed that the assessment bill implied that the civil magistrate "is a competent judge of Religious Truth or that he may employ Religion as an engine of Civil policy." Further, in the next paragraph he wrote, "Because the establishment proposed by the Bill is not requisite for the support of the Christian Religion, to say that it is, is a contradiction to the Christian Religion itself, for every page of it disavows a dependence on the powers of this world."

The years that Madison had spent at Princeton meant that he knew the history of Christianity, to which he now referred to support his arguments against the assessment bill. In the seventh paragraph he wrote, "During almost fifteen centuries has the legal establishment of Christianity been on trial. What have been its fruits? More or less in all places, pride and indolence in the Clergy, ignorance and servility in the laity, in both, superstition, bigotry and persecution." Madison enforced his argument by referring to the Constantinian symbiosis of church and state that Anabaptists and Baptists viewed as ushering in the fall of the church: "Enquire of the Teachers of Christianity for the ages in which it appeared in its greatest lustre; those of every sect, point to the ages prior to its incorporation with Civil policy." Thus to the previous arguments based on reason, French Enlightenment philosophy, theology, and practical grounds, Madison added the argument of the historical record, which to him conveyed one message: the establishment of religion, even Christianity, was an unmitigated disaster for both church and state.

Madison's masterpiece soon found its way into every county of the state. Its impact was all that Madison and

Jefferson had hoped it would be. George Nicholas and George Mason saw to it that copies were widely distributed. Mason sent a copy to George Washington with a request that he make a statement against the assessment bill, which he opposed, largely based upon the divisive nature of the issue. The Presbyterians, now thoroughly aroused over the inherent dangers in the bill, took a number of actions, each more vigorous than the previous one. Finally, in a convention called for the purpose on August 10, the Presbyterians rejected the assessment bill in unequivocal terms. There had always been those Presbyterians who were critical of the bill—like Zachariah Johnston, who was also a delegate from Augusta County to the General Assembly. In a speech he gave in 1786, Johnston reportedly said, "The very day that the Presbyterians shall be established by law and become a body politic, is the same day Zachariah Johnston will become a dissenter. Dissent from that religion I cannot in honesty, but from the establishment I will."[43] Now Johnston no longer found himself alone. Virtually all Presbyterians, ministers and laymen alike, joined the Baptists in opposing the bill. The Quakers, who had been a very silent people in Virginia with only one delegate in the House of Delegates, also joined the chorus of opposition to the assessment bill.

Although the pro-assessment forces managed to gather a thousand signatures on eleven memorials supporting the bill, the dissenters, who now included the Methodists, were able to collect twelve times that many signatures on more than one hundred petitions. One of these, known as the "formula petition," was anonymous but originated with the General Committee at its meeting in August 1785. This petition was circulated in twenty-

---

43. Johnston, cited by Buckley in *Church and State in Revolutionary Virginia: 1776-1787*, p. 104. Leland quoted Johnston in his sermon entitled "A Blow at the Root," which he delivered in Cheshire, Massachusetts, on April 9, 1801. However, there is some disagreement on exactly when Johnston delivered his speech. Leland claimed 1786, but Buckley suggested 1784, and M. W. Paxton, Johnston's biographer, thought it was 1785. See the quotation in *The Writings of John Leland*, ed. L. F. Greene (New York: Arno Press and the *New York Times*, 1969), p. 254.

nine different memorials and accumulated 4,899 signatures, far above the 1,552 signatures garnered by *A Memorial and Remonstrance.* Of this petition Thomas Buckley writes,

> The men who signed such petitions were neither rationalists nor indifferent to the progress of organized religion. Rather, they were evangelical Christians believing deeply in the principle of voluntary support. A wide gap existed between these advocates of voluntarism and the supporters of the assessment; but an even greater distance, though perhaps unrecognized at the time, separated both of these groups from those who embraced the principles of Madison and Jefferson.[44]

Buckley is certainly correct about the fundamental differences separating those "evangelicals" who opposed the assessment bill from the rationalists such as Madison and Jefferson. However, there is abundant evidence to indicate that John Leland, a most ardent admirer of Jefferson and a leading spokesman among the Baptist ministers, recognized the basic differences within the coalition that was in the process of separating church and state in Virginia and establishing religious freedom.

By the end of 1785, it was evident even to the most diehard establishmentarian that the general assessment bill was dead. Madison wrote to Jefferson, "The steps taken throughout the Country to defeat the General Assessment bill have produced all the effect that could have been wished."[45] As chairman of the Committee on the Courts of Justice, Madison proceeded to present over one hundred bills for revision of previously enacted legislation, a process that was first initiated in 1779. However, when petty opposition developed that slowed the process, Madison leaped a number of hurdles, and on December 14, 1785, he presented Jefferson's bill for the establishing of religious freedom. After the defeat of a number of amendments or alterations to the bill and even an attempt to postpone action until the next session, the bill

44. Buckley, *Church and State in Revolutionary Virginia: 1776-1787,* p. 149.
45. Madison, cited by Buckley in ibid., p. 153.

was passed 74 to 20. Madison's strategy of taking the issues to the people had triumphed, and the dissenters and their rationalist friends were jubilant.

The crucial decade for the future of church-state relations in Virginia had come to a close, but the General Committee was not yet through. It immediately launched a campaign to repeal the incorporation bill and divest the Episcopal Church of the glebes (the farms and residences purchased with tax revenues for the use of Anglican clergymen). In effect, the war was over. All that remained was a mopping-up operation in which, once again, the Baptists found themselves alone. The Baptist General Committee sent emissaries to the Presbyterians and the Methodists, seeking their support, but these efforts were unsuccessful. Both the Presbyterians and the Methodists refused to get involved. "But the Baptists," writes Garnett Ryland, "who recognized this as a final phase of their long struggle, pushed it to its logical conclusion by their persistence."[46] Finally, in January 1794, after receiving an avalanche of petitions calling for the end of the religious establishment, the General Assembly repealed every prior act dealing with religion except the Act for Establishing Religious Freedom.

The Role of Thomas Jefferson, the Rationalist

In the family cemetery on the hillside, amid the trees and just beyond the gardens of Monticello that Jefferson loved so much, stands a simple monument with the inscription "Thomas Jefferson, Author of the Declaration of Independence, of the Statute of Virginia for Religious Freedom, and Father of the University of Virginia." True, William Warren Sweet is correct when he writes, "But justice compels the admission that Jefferson's part in this accomplishment [of religious freedom] was not so great as was that of James Madison, nor were the contributions of either or both as important as was that of the humble

46. Ryland, *The Baptists of Virginia: 1699-1926*, p. 132.

people called Baptists."[47] Nevertheless, it was Jefferson's bill that established religious freedom in Virginia. Jefferson wrote the bill in 1777 and presented it to the General Assembly in 1779, where it was almost forgotten for several years thereafter—but not quite. Like Jefferson himself, it was always there in the background, poised to reappear at the right time. On December 17, 1785, after some revision, the bill "whose time had come" was passed by the General Assembly in much the same form as Jefferson had first presented it. On January 19, 1786, it became law when it was signed by the Speaker of the House.

The bill was given the title "An Act for Establishing Religious Freedom." It had three sections: the first presented a brief summary of Jefferson's argument for religious freedom; the second, the law itself; and the third, a brief commentary on the nature of legislative statutes.

Jefferson struck a rationalist note in his opening statement:

> 1. Whereas Almighty God hath created the mind free, that all attempts to influence it by temporal punishments or burthens, or by civil incapacitations, tend only to beget habits of hypocrisy and meanness, and are a departure from the plan of the Holy author of our religion to propagate it by coercions on either, as was in his Almighty power to do . . .

Jefferson brought this first section to a close with an expression of confidence in "truth" reminiscent of Roger Williams:

> . . . and finally, that truth is great and will prevail if left to herself, that she is the proper and sufficient antagonist to error, and has nothing to fear from the conflict, unless by human interposition disarmed of her natural weapons, free argument and debate, errors ceasing to be dangerous when it is permitted freely to contradict them . . .[48]

47. Sweet, *The Story of Religion in America* (New York: Harper & Row, 1950), pp. 192-93.

48. Jefferson, "An Act for Establishing Religious Freedom," in *The Papers of Thomas Jefferson*, vol. 2, ed. Julian Boyd (Princeton: Princeton University Press, 1950), pp. 545-47. For the full text of the bill, see the Appendix.

owe to our Creator, and the manner of discharging it, can be directed only by reason and conviction, not by force and violence (so fully expressed in the XVI Art. of the Bill of Rights, and the late Act for establishing Religious Liberty) we cannot see with what propriety the General Assembly could incorporate the Protestant Episcopal Church, give her a name, Describe the character of her members, modulate the forms of her government & appoint the Time and place of her meeting. If this is not done by force, what force can there be in law? and to what lengths this may lead and what violence it may produce, time only can discover, but we fear the awful consequences. The act appears a Bitumen to Cement Church and State together: the foundation for Ecclesiastical Tyranny and the first steps towards an Inquisition.[53]

Although the Baptists once again found themselves on a collision course with the Episcopalians, they could not count on either Madison or Jefferson in their new campaign. They also failed to enlist the support of either the Presbyterians or the Methodists. Nevertheless, they achieved some success: in the next year the General Assembly did repeal the incorporation act. However, it left intact the glebes, which the Baptists and the Presbyterians considered public property because they had been purchased with tax revenues. Not satisfied, both groups petitioned the assembly for the sale of the glebes. Finally, in 1799, out of deference to the persistent dissenters, Madison prodded the assembly into selling the disputed lands.[54]

At long last the General Committee was satisfied, as it had every right to be. During the years of its existence it had led the dissenters in its battles for religious liberty, battles that involved the complete disestablishment of the Protestant Episcopal Church. Its work also led to the union of the Separate and the Regular Baptists, who when joined were called the United Baptist Churches of Christ in Virginia. The committee also spoke out forcefully against slavery. Behind all these achieve-

53. Cited by Ryland in *The Baptists of Virginia: 1699-1926*, p. 128. Ryland reproduces the entire memorial on pp. 127-30.
54. Buckley, *Church and State in Revolutionary Virginia: 1776-1787*, p. 172.

ments was the influence of the most important political thinker and activist among Virginia Baptists, Reverend John Leland, who became the liaison on behalf of the Baptists between both Jefferson and Madison.

Known in American history for his friendship with Jefferson and the mammoth cheese from Cheshire, Massachusetts, that he presented to the president, Leland's importance lies in his participation in the struggle for religious freedom in Virginia and Massachusetts, and his agitation for a bill of rights.

Chapter VII

Of Revival, Politics,
and the First Amendment

In the pivotal year of 1785, revival came once again to Virginia. Perhaps the foregleams of the Second Great Awakening, the revival continued unabated until 1791 or 1792, bringing new religious life and greatly increasing the membership of all three of the major dissenting denominations.[1] John Leland was disappointed, however, that there were relatively few young men who "felt the call into the ministry" as a result of this resurgence of interest in spiritual concerns. Primarily an itinerant evangelist in whose soul the fires of the First Great Awakening still burned, Leland later recalled in his autobiography some of those stirring events in which he had played a part: "When the work seemed to languish in one neighborhood, it would break out in another, and consequently, there was a continual fall of heavenly rain from October, 1787, until March, 1789, during which time I baptized about 400. Precisely 300 of them were baptized in 1788—more than I have ever baptized in any other year."[2]

1. Robert Baylor Semple, *History of the Baptists in Virginia,* first published in 1810, revised and extended by G. W. Beale (Lafayette, Tenn.: Church History Research and Archives, 1976), p. 58.
2. *The Writings of John Leland,* ed. L. F. Greene (New York: Arno Press and the *New York Times,* 1969), p. 27.

Before he left Virginia, Leland reported having baptized exactly 700 new converts. He left behind two rather sizeable churches that he had organized, one in Orange County and the other in Louisa County. His moving from Virginia to New England seems not to have changed his priorities or his life-style—only his geographic location. He continued his itinerant ministry and his crusade for complete religious freedom, the two chief passions of his life. However, his literary output increased considerably. From this period date most of his published tracts and political addresses.

JOHN LELAND, 1754-1841

Leland was born in Grafton, Massachusetts, on May 14, 1754. Since his father entertained serious doubts about the validity of infant baptism, John was not baptized until he was three years old. However, it was a never-to-be-forgotten experience, because he ran out of the house to escape the ordeal and in the process fell down and bloodied his nose. "All the merit of this transaction," he wrote later, "I must give to the maid who caught me, my father and the minister; for I was not a voluntary candidate, but a reluctant subject, forced against my will."[3] Naturally, such an experience did nothing to further his spiritual development.

According to Leland, he was a profligate youth until he was eighteen, when he suddenly lost his desire for the pleasures of this world and began to attend every religious meeting in the vicinity of Grafton. Immersing himself in the study of Scripture, he spent about fifteen months wrestling with his sins and his doubts. At twenty, he began ever so hesitantly to exhort others. He was like Isaac Backus in two respects: he left the Congregationalists for the Baptists, and although his formal education was meager, his gifts were considerable. Perhaps he hesitated to embark on a ministerial career because of his lack of education and his "rustic manners." Apparently he never felt at ease

3. Ibid., p. 10.

among the better educated and more sophisticated of his peers. However, his rural background well equipped him to communicate the gospel in revolutionary Virginia, and his firm faith and sense of humor enabled him to survive.

After visiting Virginia in 1775, he returned to Massachusetts to claim Sally Devine of Hopkinton as his bride. Together they left their native state for Culpeper County, Virginia, where the young minister accepted a call to the Mountponey Church, which was a member of the Ketocton Association, a group of regular Baptist churches in fellowship with one another. Here he was ordained without the laying on of hands, which soon became a source of controversy in the association. After leaving that church in 1779, he submitted to another ordination with the laying on of hands, which indicates something of the spirit of the man. (The second ordination took place on June 24, 1786; the laying on of hands was done by a presbytery.)

Considered a country bumpkin by his enemies and somewhat eccentric by his friends, he was indeed a rugged individualist, even among Baptists, but utterly honest and self-effacing.[4] Leland's interests went far beyond those of his own denomination; his was not a sectarian spirit. He hinted at this side of himself in his willingness to be ordained a second time, about which he wrote, "By this, not only a union took place between myself and others, but it was a small link in the chain of events, which produced a union among all the Baptists in Virginia, not long afterwards."[5]

Leland returned to New England in 1791. Apparently he was content with the momentum that was moving Virginia toward the sale of the glebes, which he saw as necessary for the complete disestablishment of the Episcopal Church. Then, too, the revival fires had begun to burn low in Virginia, and Leland, ever restless for new challenges, felt the call to return to his home country. He and his large family first moved to Connecticut, and by 1792 had settled in Cheshire, Massachusetts. Soon afterward

4. See J. Bradley Creed, "American Prophet of Religious Individualism," Ph.D. diss., Southwestern Baptist Theological Seminary, 1986.
5. *The Writings of John Leland*, p. 26.

Leland joined forces with Isaac Backus to help pull down the Congregational establishment. Unlike Backus, Leland did live to see Massachusetts give up "her establishment." In working against it he wrote some of his most forceful tracts and delivered possibly his most effective addresses on religious freedom and the separation of church and state. His most important treatise on the subject, entitled *The Rights of Conscience Inalienable*, was published in New London, Connecticut, shortly after his return from Virginia in 1791. In addition to waging this battle, Leland continued his itinerant ministry without slackening his pace until age and infirmity stopped him.

Leland rejoiced that the federal Constitution made it possible for a "Pagan, Turk, Jew or Christian" to be eligible for any post in the government.[6] In much of his work he sounded the familiar themes of Jefferson and Madison, but his position was grounded in the example and teachings of Jesus Christ:

> I now call for an instance, where Jesus Christ, the author of his religion, or the apostles, who were divinely inspired, ever gave orders to, or intimated, that the civil powers on earth, ought to force people to observe the rules and doctrine of the gospel.
>
> Mahomet called in the use of the law and sword, to convert people to his religion; but Jesus did not—does not.
>
> It is the duty of men to love God with all their hearts, and their neighbors as themselves; but have legislatures authority to punish men if they do not; so there are many things that Jesus and the apostles taùght, that men ought to obey, which yet the civil law has no concern in.[7]

By 1831, Leland had apparently despaired of seeing Massachusetts give up "her establishment"; on June 17 of that year he wrote to Reverend S. M. Noel, "For more than half a century, I have been trying to do a little for Him who has done so much for me; but now the time is gone and nothing has been done as I hoped. I die a debtor; let me then die a beggar."[8] However,

---

6. Ibid., p. 191.
7. Ibid., p. 187.
8. Leland, cited by L. H. Butterfield in *Elder John Leland, Jeffersonian Itinerant* (New York: Arno Press, 1980), p. 240.

Leland lived ten more years, long enough to see Massachusetts give up the Congregational establishment, which by that time had become largely Unitarian. On January 14, 1841, a few days after preaching his last sermon, he died in North Adams, Massachusetts. Engraved on his tombstone is the epitaph he had written himself: "Here lies the body of John Leland, who labored [sixty-seven] years to promote piety, and vindicate the civil and religious rights of all men." The order of these phrases is significant, indicating that Leland considered himself first and foremost a minister of the gospel and only secondarily a political activist. Although his importance in the struggle for religious freedom in Virginia and the nation lay in his role as a statesman, his political activity was both inspired and informed by his religious commitment. This first became evident in his relationship with the General Committee.

THE GENERAL COMMITTEE, 1784-1799

The General Committee was formed in 1784 to coordinate the political activities of the Baptists in Virginia. Although petitions had been sent to the House of Burgesses and its successor, the General Assembly, for more than fifteen years, the results had been less than satisfying as far as the Baptists were concerned. Legal persecution had ceased and dissent had been decriminalized, but ministers of dissenting denominations still could not perform legal marriages. Presbyterians and Baptists often claimed that they did not enjoy full citizenship in the commonwealth. The Baptists in particular were the objects of ridicule and discrimination. The Methodists fared little better, although they were technically a branch of the Protestant Episcopal Church until 1785. The Mennonites and Quakers, who were also committed to religious freedom and the separation of church and state, were considered no threat to the status quo.

The General Committee was established to make more effective the dissenters' campaign for complete religious freedom in Virginia. Although it was made up of four representatives from

160

each of the four Baptist associations in Virginia, the committee envisioned its task in something other than sectarian terms, as indicated by its overtures to both the Presbyterians and the Methodists to join the committee in its efforts.

The committee was formed in 1784, and Leland's name first appeared in its proceedings in 1786, when he and Reuben Ford, onetime clerk of the committee, were charged with the responsibility of taking a memorial to the General Assembly. Generally speaking, Reuben Ford appeared before the General Assembly on behalf of the committee. Apparently Leland was made an agent of the committee along with Ford because the memorial was largely his composition. The language, the ideas, and the logic all seem to indicate this.

The memorial began by reminding the delegates that upon the basis of the promise of religious liberty embodied in the Virginia Bill of Rights, Baptists had taken the oath of allegiance to the new government and had supported the revolutionary cause. Therefore, they had been led to believe that in adopting Article XVI, the General Assembly intended to abide by its provisions. But such was not the case. The incorporation act had not only indicated that the Baptists' interpretation of Article XVI differed from that of the General Assembly; it had disappointed and alarmed them. Since Jefferson's bill had just been passed by the assembly, the memorial referred to it in one of its principal declarations: "If truth is great, and will prevail if left to itself (as declared in the Act Establishing Religious Freedom), we wish it may be so left, which is the only way to convince the gazing world that Disciples do not follow Christ for Loaves, and that Preachers do not preach for Benefices."[9]

After alluding to the changing character of the Church of England from Edward VI to Charles II in 1661, the memorial pointed out that since the king of England was the head of the Church of England, "Our declaration of Independence appears

---

9. Cited by Garnett Ryland in *The Baptists of Virginia: 1699-1926* (Richmond: Virginia Baptist Board of Missions and Education, 1955), p. 129.

to have made every Son of Liberty in America a Dissenter from that Church."[10]

The inescapable logic of this unusually long petition led the General Committee to the following conclusion:

> If the members of the Protestant Episcopal Church prefer Episcopacy to any other form of Government, they have an undoubted Right as free Citizens of the State to enjoy it. But to call in the aid of legislature to Establish it threatens the freedom of Religious Liberty in its Consequences. And, whereas, the Incorporating Act appears to be pregnant with evil and dangerous to religious Liberty, your Petitioners humbly remonstrate against it; and trust that the wisdom of our Hon. House will repeal the exceptionable parts of the said Act and apply the property to the use of the community in such a manner as to you shall seem just.[11]

The memorial had an effect, albeit a limited one. In August 1787 Ford and Leland reported to the General Committee that the General Assembly had repealed the incorporation act but that the glebes had been left untouched. From that time on, one of the concerns that the members of the General Committee addressed annually was the sale of the "vacant glebes." But there were other matters that soon compelled the attention of the committee, foremost of which was the new federal Constitution drawn up by the Constitutional Convention.

On March 7, 1788, the General Committee met in Williams' Meeting House in Goochland County, where John Waller was pastor.[12] This turned out to be one of the more fruitful meetings of the committee. The first question entertained was this: "Whether the new Federal Constitution, which had now lately made its appearance in public, made sufficient provision for the secure enjoyment of religious liberty; on which, it was

10. Ibid.
11. Ibid.
12. Because of his faith, Waller had suffered both imprisonment and beatings at the hands of the sheriff and parish priest. For a detailed account of the trials and suffering Waller endured for preaching the gospel, see Lewis Peyton Little, *Imprisoned Preachers and Religious Liberty in Virginia* (Lynchburg, Va.: J. P. Bell Co., Inc., 1938), pp. 229-33.

agreed unanimously that, in the opinion of the General Committee, it did not."[13]

The committee also agreed to petition the General Assembly again "asking the sale of the vacant glebes as being public property; and accordingly four persons were chosen from the General Committee to present their memorial, viz.: Eli Clay, Reuben Ford, John Waller and John Williams."[14] The remainder of the meeting was taken up with correspondence from various Baptist leaders from the North whom Leland was asked to visit "if convenient." A resolution on slavery was adopted, but its submission was postponed until the next meeting of the committee.

When the General Committee met in August, it was quite evident that Leland had emerged as the most forceful leader among his peers. First, he was chosen along with Waller and Clay to formulate the memorial on the glebe lands. Second, when James Manning of Rhode Island College (which became Brown University) wrote encouraging the General Committee to take the lead in establishing a seminary for the training of ministers, Leland was named to the nine-member committee to consider the matter. Third, it was Leland who offered the resolution on slavery that was adopted:

> Resolved, That slavery is a violent deprivation of the rights of nature and inconsistent with a republican government, and therefore recommend it to our brethren to make use of every legal measure to extirpate this horrid evil from the land; and pray Almighty God that our honorable Legislature may have it in their power to proclaim the great Jubilee, consistent with the principles of good policy.[15]

At the same meeting, Leland and John Williams were charged with the responsibility of compiling a history of the Baptists of Virginia—yet another indication of Leland's prominence. Although this task was apparently put aside while more pressing

13. Cited by Semple in *History of the Baptists in Virginia*, p. 102.
14. Ibid., pp. 102-3.
15. Ibid., p. 105.

matters were pursued, eventually it bore fruit: Robert Baylor Semple's *History of the Baptists in Virginia,* which was first published in 1810, owes its inception to the action of the General Committee.

JAMES MADISON AND THE FIRST AMENDMENT

The more pressing matter to which Leland turned his attention was the federal Constitution. Article VI was the only clause that related to religion. While the Constitution prohibited administering religious tests to applicants for federal office, Leland and his colleagues were not satisfied. Since Leland lived in Orange County, which was the home of James Madison, the mounting opposition to the Constitution led by Leland and another prominent minister by the name of Aaron Bledsoe became a matter of grave concern to Madison's friends and relatives.

The fall and winter of 1787-88 found Madison a busy man. On September 17, 1787, he, along with the other members of the Constitutional Convention, signed the revolutionary document. He then joined Alexander Hamilton and John Jay in issuing the *Federalist* papers, which Hamilton had conceived in order to rally support for the new federal Constitution. The smaller states were running into little difficulty in the ratification process, but New York and Virginia were the two states where the opposition against the Constitution as it stood—without a bill of rights—was most formidable. Hamilton saw no need for a bill of rights, because he believed, as he argued in *The Federalist, No. 84,* that the proposed constitution contained provisions for protecting all necessary human rights.[16] However, the opposition that Hamilton faced in New York was considerably different from that which confronted Madison in Virginia. At the heart of the problem for the Leland-led forces

16. *Selections from The Federalist: A Commentary on the Constitution of the United States,* ed. Henry S. Commager (Arlington Heights, Ill.: Harlan Davidson, Inc., 1949), pp. 134-37.

was the lack of a sufficient guarantee for religious freedom in the new constitution.

The situation presented something of a crisis for Madison. It was commonly believed that if New York and Virginia failed to ratify the Constitution, other states would follow suit, and the results could be disastrous. Up until this point Madison had preferred and intended to keep his distance from any controversy. After all, he was the Constitution's major author, and he felt, as Hamilton did, that no bill of rights was necessary. But a number of letters from family and friends forced him to change his plans and eventually his mind.

As early as January 30, Madison's father informed him of the rising opposition to ratification in Orange County. He wrote that a Colonel Thomas Barbour had declared himself a candidate from Orange County to the ratifying convention, and the colonel had the support of the Baptists, who were generally opposed to ratification. James Gordon, Jr., who had also announced himself a candidate but one in favor of ratification, urged Madison to return to Virginia "without delay," because "the loss of the constitution in this state may involve consequences the most alarming to every citizen of America."[17]

Perhaps the letter that most influenced Madison to rethink his course of action came from a Revolutionary War officer, a Captain Joseph Spencer. Spencer had been imprisoned in Orange County in 1773 "for a breach of good behavior in teaching and preaching the gospel as a Baptist not having a license."[18] Spencer, doubtless a sincere layman, indicated that he had a low opinion of Colonel Barbour and his tactics in using the Baptists to promote himself and his campaign. But the heart of Baptist dissatisfaction with the Constitution was another thing: "The Preachers of that Society are much alarm'd fearing Religious Liberty is not Sufficiently secur'd. They pretend to other objections but that I think is the principle objection, could that be remov'd by someone capable of the Task, I think they

17. Gordon, cited by Butterfield in *Elder John Leland*, p. 186.
18. Little, *Imprisoned Preachers and Religious Liberty in Virginia*, p. 380.

would become friends to it, that body of people has become very formidible in point of Elections."[19]

Spencer also suggested that since Leland's home was on the way to Madison's from Fredricksburg, Madison should take the time "to spend a few hours in his company." In addition, Spencer enclosed a copy of Leland's objections to the federal Constitution, a copy that was sent to Barbour at the colonel's request. It is an interesting list of ten articles, ranging from criticism of the proposed organization of Congress in two houses instead of one, to criticism of the lack of an adequate guarantee of freedom of the press in Article VIII. It is quite evident that what set Leland's call for a bill of rights apart from some other similar calls was his declaration of the need for a legal guarantee of complete religious liberty backed by no establishment of religion. The first and last articles spelled this out most clearly:

> 1st. There is no Bill of Rights. Whenever a number of men enter into a state of Society, a Number of individual Rights must be given up to Society, but there should be a memorial of those not surrendered, otherwise every natural & domestic Right become[s] alienable, which raises Tyranny at once, and this is as necessary in one Form of Government as in another.
>
> 10ly. What is clearest of all—Religious Liberty, is not sufficiently secured. No Religious test is Required as qualification to fill any office under the United States, but if a Majority of Congress with the President favour one System more than another, they may oblige all others to pay to the support of their System as much as they please, and if Oppression does not ensue, it will be owing to the Mildness of Administration, and not to any Constitutional defense, and if the manners of people are so far Corrupted, that they cannot live by Republican principles, it is Very Dangerous leaving Religious Liberty at their Mercy.[20]

It is probable that Madison did confer with Leland a few days before the election, in which Madison won a seat in the

19. Spencer, cited by Butterfield in *Elder John Leland*, p. 186.
20. All ten articles and Spencer's letter, part of the Madison Papers in the Library of Congress, are reproduced in full by Butterfield in *Elder John Leland*, pp. 185-88. For the complete text, see the Appendix.

ratifying convention by a slight majority over his nearest rival. That legendary meeting has sparked several different recountings of it; the details of the event are somewhat obscure, and whether or not the meeting actually took place is still a matter of debate among historians.[21] In any case, Madison and Leland, who were not personally acquainted before March 20, became friends. Evidence of this new relationship is seen in the subsequent correspondence of the two men. For example, upon the eve of his departure for Congress on July 6, Madison wrote his father and sent him two copies of *The Federalist*, "one for Mr. Leland and the other for Mr. Bledsoe."[22]

Patrick Henry had failed to exploit the discontent of the Baptists and others in his attempt to defeat Madison's bid for election to the ratifying convention. However, he did keep Madison out of the Senate and tried to block his election to the House of Representatives. In the process he continued to argue that Madison still saw no need for a bill of rights. George Eve, pastor of the Blue Run Baptist Church in Orange County, made a trip to Montpelier to question Madison personally about Henry's allegations. Madison made his position a matter of record when he wrote to Eve on January 2, 1789, saying that he had "never seen in the constitution as it now stands those serious dangers which have alarmed many respectable citizens," and therefore he had supported ratification of the Constitution without amendments, but that "circumstances are now changed."[23] He continued,

21. Butterfield examines the evidence for and against the alleged meeting of Leland and Madison at Gum Springs (now the Leland-Madison Park) and concludes that the circumstantial evidence suggesting such a meeting is very strong, as is the local tradition, which was very much alive at the time of Madison's death in 1836. Butterfield writes, "There can be no question that the monument [at the park] memorializes an actual occurrence" (*Elder John Leland*, pp. 188, 195). In *A History of Baptists in Virginia*, Reuben Edward Alley writes, "Evidence is totally lacking that Madison was dependent upon Leland for election to the Virginia convention in June 1788" ([Richmond: Virginia Baptist General Board, 1973], p. 118). For a discussion of the Madison-Leland relationship, see pp. 115-18 of Alley's book.

22. Madison, cited by Butterfield in *Elder John Leland*, p. 192.

23. Ibid., pp. 192-93.

It is my sincere opinion that the Constitution ought to be revised, and that the first Congress . . . ought to prepare and recommend to the States for ratification, the most satisfactory provisions for all essential rights, particularly the rights of conscience in the fullest latitude, the freedom of the press, trial by jury, security against general warrants, etc.[24]

Eve shared his proof of Madison's change of mind with his Baptist friends. This time there was no question about Baptists' support of Madison. Their doubts about the statesman's commitment to religious freedom were evidently alleviated. After Madison's election to the House of Representatives, Leland wrote a letter congratulating him and also requesting information about the financial solvency of the new nation that he could not obtain "without the aid of a particular friend." He also expressed a desire to examine all the laws forthcoming, stressing what was uppermost in his mind: "One Thing I shall expect; that if religious Liberty is anywise threatened, that I shall receive the earliest Intelligence. I take the Liberty of writing this to you, lest I should not be at Home when you pass by on your way to Congress."[25]

Those who had staked their hopes on Madison's integrity and commitment to freedom of religion were not disappointed. On June 7, 1789, Madison, considering himself "bound in honor and in duty," submitted the first version of the no-establishment clause of an amendment that after ratification became the First Amendment in the Bill of Rights.[26]

It would be a mistake to leave the impression that the Leland-led dissenters were the only ones insisting upon a bill of rights, but they were among the most significant complainants. True, Jefferson had written from Paris to say that the Constitution was incomplete without a bill of rights, and Patrick Henry

24. Ibid., p. 193.
25. Leland, in a letter from the undated Madison Papers, cited by Butterfield in ibid., p. 194.
26. Originally twelve amendments, this one being the third among them, were submitted for ratification in 1791, but the first two were not ratified; thus the amendment containing the no-establishment clause became the First Amendment.

had been saying the same thing for some time (although his motives were suspect, and thus Madison had ignored his call for a bill of rights). However, after the political and personal motives had been accounted for in the ground swell of discontent over the prospect of a constitution without a bill of rights, the Baptists constituted a hard core of resistance on the basis of principle.

Continuing to press its cause, the General Committee asked John Leland to write a letter to George Washington on its behalf, to be signed by its officers. Therefore, on August 8, 1789, Leland wrote,

> When the Constitution first made its appearance in Virginia, we, as a society, had unusual strugglings of mind, fearing that the liberty of conscience, dearer to us than property or life, was not sufficiently secured. Perhaps our jealousies were heightened by the usage we received in Virginia, under the regal government when mobs, fines, bonds, and prisons were our frequent repast.
>
> Convinced, on the one hand, that without an effective National Government, the States would fall into disunion and all the consequent evils; and on the other hand, fearing that we should be accessory to some religious oppression, should any one society in the Union preponderate over the rest; yet, amidst all these inquietudes of mind, our consolation arose from this consideration,—the plan must be good, for it has the signature of a tried, trusty friend, and if religious liberty is rather insecure in the Constitution, "the Administration will certainly prevent all oppression, for a Washington will preside."[27]

Since there was as yet no federal bill of rights, the General Committee sought to put pressure on Washington by reminding him that they still believed the Constitution was flawed, although they had confidence in Washington as a defender of religious freedom. In his reply Washington assured the General Committee that he too would support the establishing of "effectual barriers against the horrors of spiritual tyranny, and every species of religious persecution":

27. *The Writings of John Leland*, p. 53.

If I could have entertained the slightest apprehension that the Constitution framed by the Convention where I had the honor to preside, might possibly endanger the religious rights of any ecclesiastical society, certainly I would never have placed my signature to it; and if I could now conceive that the general government might even be so administered, as to render the liberty of conscience insecure, I beg you will be persuaded, that no one would be more zealous than myself, to establish effectual barriers against the horrors of spiritual tyranny, and every species of religious persecution.[28]

While the Baptists were grateful for the sentiments Washington expressed, they still insisted that Article VI of the Constitution, which prohibited congress from administering religious tests to those seeking "any office or public trust under the United States," left the door open for imposing such tests for purposes not specified.

Much was accomplished during the six weeks that followed the committee's lodging of its complaint. After Madison's no-establishment clause underwent much debate and several revisions in both houses of congress, Madison was appointed to serve on the Conference Committee, which came up with the final version approved by the House of Representatives on September 24 and by the Senate on the following day, despite the open opposition of its members from Massachusetts and Connecticut. The First Amendment in its final form read, "Congress shall make no law respecting an establishment of religion, or prohibiting the free exercise thereof, or abridging the freedom of speech or of the press, or the right of the people peaceably to assemble and to petition the government for the redress of grievances."[29]

At last the Baptists of Virginia were satisfied. In a letter of November 20, 1789, Madison informed Washington, "One of the principal leaders of the Baptists lately sent me word that the

28. Washington, cited in *The Writings of John Leland*, pp. 54-55.
29. For the sequence of events from the introduction of the First Amendment to its final passage, see Edwin S. Gaustad, *Faith of Our Fathers: Religion and the New Nation* (San Francisco: Harper & Row, 1987), pp. 156-68.

amendments had entirely satisfied the disaffected of his sect and that it would appear in their subsequent conduct."[30] At last the legal battle had been won, and the cherished principle of religious liberty and the institutional separation of church and state were now enshrined in the Constitution and its Bill of Rights.

All the states except Massachusetts and Connecticut ratified the Bill of Rights before the end of 1791. This fact may have compelled Leland, who had played such a significant role in the struggle in Virginia, to leave Virginia for New England to join Isaac Backus in completing an unfinished task.

COMMON CAUSE

"Dissenting Protestantism," as William Lee Miller has called it, made common cause with rationalism and deism to bring about a revolution within the Revolution. The coalition thus formed functioned effectively despite basic theological and philosophical differences, as William Warren Sweet and Sidney Mead pointed out years ago.[31] If either side in this coalition had been missing, the cause almost surely would have failed—at least until the unbridled religious pluralism of the new nation would have demanded some kind of accommodation. However, as this work has attempted to demonstrate, religious freedom guaranteed by the institutional separation of church and state was not primarily the result of a practical solution to an indissoluble problem but the outworking of a basic theological principle rooted in the gospel of the "twice born," a gospel that had found its earliest expression in the Reformation of the sixteenth century among the Con-

30. Joseph Martin Dawson cites this letter in *Baptists and the American Republic* (Nashville: Broadman Press, 1956), p. 115.
31. See William Warren Sweet, *The Story of Religion in America* (New York: Harper & Row, 1950), pp. 189-95; and Sidney Mead, *The Lively Experiment* (New York: Harper & Row, 1963), p. 43.

tinental evangelical Anabaptists and their English counter-parts.[32]

Even though Miller is correct when he attributes the ground swell of religious liberty in the colonies to "dissenting Protestantism" rather than to the French Enlightenment, Edwin Gaustad reminds us that dissenting Protestantism alone could not have "stormed the gates of the establishment." He continues, "More power was required, more troops needed to bring down alliances of church and state, for behind those alliances stood all the force of history, all the authority of received wisdom, all the assurance of axiomatic truth."[33] One need look no further than a simple comparison of Virginia with Massachusetts and Connecticut: despite the success of the Leland-led dissenters in Virginia, the Backus-led forces failed to bring down the establishment or achieve religious freedom in Massachusetts and Connecticut. The one element missing in Massachusetts and Connecticut that was present in Virginia was statesmen of the stature of Madison and Jefferson committed to religious freedom.

Madison and Jefferson were as indispensable to the imbuing of these concepts into the law of the land as the dissenters were indispensable to the task of engraving these concepts upon the minds and hearts of the people. The two men worked in complementary fashion: Jefferson was primarily the philosopher and Madison the architect.

In writing to the Danbury Baptist Association in Connecticut on July 1, 1802, Jefferson explicitly identified with the Baptist understanding of the no-establishment clause of the First Amendment by using the analogy of a wall:

> Believing with you that religion is a matter which lies solely between man & his god, that he owes account to none other for his faith or his worship, that the legitimate powers of government reach actions only and not opinions, I contemplate with sovereign reverence that act of the whole American people which

32. For a succinct summary of the religious dimensions of this struggle, see William Lee Miller, *The First Liberty: Religion and the American Republic* (New York: Alfred A. Knopf, 1986), p. 153.
33. Gaustad, *Faith of Our Fathers*, p. 34.

declared that *their* legislature should make no law respecting an establishment of religion, or prohibiting the free exercise thereof; thus building a wall of separation between church and state.[34]

If Jefferson personified the Enlightenment, Leland, his friend and admirer, was the personal embodiment of dissenting Protestantism, to use Miller's term. Even though some dissenters may have failed to see a difference between their call for religious freedom and that of the rationalists, this was not true of Leland. True, he sounded very much like Jefferson when he wrote that it was not within the province of government "to establish fixed holy days for divine worship." But he distinguished himself from Jefferson when he explained why:

> As the appointment of such days is no part of human legislation, so the breach of the Sabbath (so called) is no part of civil jurisdiction. I am not an enemy to holy days, (the duties of religion cannot well be performed without fixed times), but these times should be fixed by the mutual agreement of religious societies, according to the word of God, and not by civil authority.[35]

This statement contains a clue to the basic ideas shaping Leland's thought. His authority was not reason—although he did not disparage reason—but God. He believed that the wellsprings of the Christian life were internal and spiritual, not subject to manmade laws. This is further borne out in the stalwart preacher's many sermons and tracts. Take the sermon entitled "A Blow at the Root," which he delivered at Cheshire, Massachusetts, on April 9, 1801. In this sermon he praised Jefferson and unleashed a scathing attack upon the Standing Order, in the process putting the triumph of religious freedom in perspective: "Let us adore that God who has been so favorable to our land, and nation—praise him for all that is past—trust him for all that is to come, and not ascribe that to man which is due to God alone."[36]

34. Jefferson, cited by Dawson in *Baptists and the American Republic*, p. 38.
35. *The Writings of John Leland*, p. 119.
36. Ibid., p. 255.

173

In an oration that he delivered on July 5, 1802, in Cheshire to celebrate the Declaration of Independence, Leland delineated the differences between the Federalist party and the Republican party (Jeffersonian Democrats), in the process indicating that he saw quite clearly the basic theological differences separating him and Jefferson:

> The federal party includes the old tories—those who admire a state-established religion, and a few others. The republican class contains those who fought, not only to be independent of Britain, but also from that policy which governs her—those who contend for the civil and religious rights of all men, and some beside. As Deism is an opinion about religion, and not so much connected with government, the Deists might be left out of the question. However, as they are not omitted, they shall here be considered. The federalists and Deists agree in one point, viz: they both believe that if Christianity is not protected by law, it will fall to the ground. But then they disagree in their wishes: the federalists wish that what they call Christianity may stand, but the Deists wish it might fall. The republicans and Deists agree in the counterpart, viz, that it would be delivering the world from one of its greatest curses, to have all legal establishments of religion abolished: but their conclusions are diametrically opposed to each other. Republicans believe that pure Christianity would gain much by such a dissolution, but the Deists suppose it would utterly fall. As for a religion of cruelty, laws to enforce it, and the steady habits of persecution, the republicans do wish to undermine them, and if Deists unite with them in this wish, they are so far right. It is true, there are some who call themselves republicans, who supposed that religion is an object of civil government, and under its control, but such men hold with the hare and run with the hound, and how they can reconcile the business of fighting with the dog and whipping the cat at the same time, I know not.[37]

It is clear from this quotation that Leland had no illusions about the motives underlying Jefferson's—and Madison's—commitment to religious liberty and the separation of church and state. Yet his friendship with both remained firm

37. Ibid., pp. 263-64.

even after he left Virginia, as his correspondence indicates. It is also evident that Leland, while not blind to the fact that all Republicans were not committed to the separation of church and state, was a Republican. Accordingly, he recognized the necessity of participating in the political process in a democratic society even though the situation was less than ideal. Perhaps this is the reason why he argued that Baptists should not hesitate to bear arms in defense of the country. Upon the same occasion, he argued that to contend for religious freedom and the rights of conscience gave no license for irresponsible citizenship:

> Gentlemen, you have taken notice that some men are always contending for the *energy of government*, while others are pleading for the *rights of the people*. On this I shall remark that man has no *right* which stands in opposition to his *social duties*; no right to exercise his liberty to destroy the right and property of his neighbor; no right that frees him from his proportionable part of the burdens of government, and restraints of just laws.[38]

Eventually Massachusetts and Connecticut did give up the establishment of religion, and probably most Congregationalists as well as dissenters were willing to say with Lyman Beecher, who had opposed the disestablishment with all his might, "That which I thought was the worst thing that could happen has turned out to be the best thing that ever happened in the state of Connecticut."[39]

IN RETROSPECT

The bicentennial of the First Amendment to the Constitution provides an opportunity to reflect upon its benefits despite what its detractors might say. In retrospect, it is almost impossible to

38. Ibid., p. 266.
39. Beecher, cited by Dawson in *Baptists and the American Republic*, p. 129.

imagine our world without the kind of freedoms spelled out in the Bill of Rights, the influence of which is beyond computation. In his introductory statement to *The Declaration on Religious Freedom (Dignitatis Humanae Personae)* of Vatican II, John Courtney Murray, a prominent American Jesuit priest, expresses this viewpoint when he writes,

> It can hardly be maintained that the Declaration [of the Vatican] is a milestone in human history—moral, political, or intellectual. The principle of religious freedom has long been recognized in constitutional law, to the point where even Marxist-Leninist political ideology is obliged to pay lip-service to it. In all honesty it must be admitted that the Church is late in acknowledging the validity of the principle.[40]

The *Declaration on Religious Freedom* of Vatican II was truly remarkable in the light of previous papal pronouncements. Among these, the pronouncements of Pius IX, issued less than a century before the convening of Vatican II, are the most famous. On December 8, 1864, the pope issued the encyclical *Quanta cura* and his *Syllabus of Errors.* In both documents he condemned religious liberty and the separation of church and state.[41] The Declaration contains the same mixture of Enlightenment thought and theological insights that marked the struggle for religious liberty in the colonies which culminated in the First Amendment. Chapter 2, entitled "Religious Freedom in the Light of Revelation," bears this out, particularly in section 12:

> The Church therefore is being faithful to the truth of the gospel, and is following the way of Christ and the apostles when she recognizes, and gives support to, the principles of religious freedom as befitting the dignity of man and as being in accord with divine revelation. Throughout the ages, the Church has kept

40. Murray, *The Declaration on Religious Freedom*, in *The Documents of Vatican II*, ed. Walter M. Abbott and Joseph Gallagher (New York: Guild Press, 1966), p. 673.

41. See *The Papal Encyclicals in Their Historical Context*, ed. Anne Fremantle (New York: New American Library, 1963), pp. 135-52.

safe and handed on the doctrine received from the Master and from the apostles. In the life of the people of God as it has made its pilgrim way through the vicissitudes of human history, there have at times appeared ways of acting which were less in accord with the spirit of the gospel and even opposed to it. Nevertheless, the doctrine of the Church that no one is to be coerced into faith has always stood firm.[42]

Franklin H. Littell, distinguished church historian and internationally recognized ecumenical leader, was asked to write a Protestant response to the Declaration. After pointing out both its strengths and its limitations, Littell touches on the significance of the American experience of religious freedom:

The American experience of religious freedom is not only an advance in Church history: it is also an important breakthrough in government. Governments which claim to achieve ultimate aims, which pretend to be more than human instruments to effect limited and specific purposes—whether "sacral" in the old sense, or "ideological" in the sense of contemporary fascism and communism—are theologically disobedient and historically retrogressive. "Secularized" governmental institutions, always to be distinguished from the state committed to secularism as an ideology, have in our situation proved beneficial to both religion and politics.[43]

In the closing paragraph of his response, which constitutes more of a commentary upon the American experience than upon the *Declaration on Religious Freedom*, Littell has written what constitutes an appropriate commentary on this study:

The assertion of religious freedom, therefore, which begins as a religious understanding and obligation, ends by giving a new institutional formation to the world. As so often has happened in the works of Christ, the work begun among the faithful is completed in the reshaping of the created order. Religious freedom, in sum, makes not only a better Church and a finer obedience among Christians: its constitutional recognition and

42. *The Documents of Vatican II*, p. 692.
43. Littell, in ibid., p. 700.

177

protection also makes a better government. Thus again, in the end, God's will for the realm of redemption and His purpose for the created order blend in a final harmony.[44]

CONCLUSION

That which made the American Revolution both unique and lasting was the Constitution and the Bill of Rights. Basic to all else that follows in the Bill of Rights is the First Amendment, which was the result of a revolution within the Revolution sparked by the "twice born." At every point in the struggle for religious freedom in the colonies, the Baptists led the way. They and those who joined them in the final phase of the battle shaped a nation of freedom. In no other country have Christianity and Judaism enjoyed such growth and influence so remarkably free from religious strife. Consequently, America has become the refuge for the persecuted of the earth, as well as a center of missionary outreach unprecedented in the history of Christianity. It would be tragic indeed if present-day evangelicals of the New Right or the mainline denominations would seek to jettison the First Amendment out of a fear of freedom.

Instead of blaming the First Amendment for the moral degeneracy of modern society, perhaps critics of the amendment should examine the nature of the church in America. As Richard John Neuhaus has pointed out in *The Naked Public Square*, the mainline denominations that once helped to set the moral standards of society have themselves fallen victim to the unbelief of the age. The New Religious Right seems to have lost its way in its attempt to court the powers of this world. The moral failure of modern society, as evidenced by the dissolution of the family, drug addiction, sexual immorality accompanied by wholesale abortion, and white-collar crime, is not the result of the freedom provided by the Constitution and the Bill of

44. Ibid.

Rights, but rather a consequence of the failure of those who are called in the name of Christ to live out the gospel as committed disciples both within the community of faith of which they are a part and within the society in which they are called upon to act out their faith.

It is still the believer, convinced of the truth of his or her message, who becomes "the salt, light, and leaven" of any society. Thus the kingdom is not brought about by the force of law or the arm of flesh but by the power of God, who still uses believers "redeemed by the blood of the Lamb" to permeate every aspect of life and to penetrate the dark corners of this world with the light of the gospel. Surely in this new era of freedom the future belongs to those who do not fear what freedom may bring but who welcome the new day of opportunity to make disciples who will also bear the truth claims of Christ to those who still wait in the darkness of human depravity and sin.

Appendix

Documents Pertaining to the Struggle
for Religious Freedom in Virginia

Letter of John Waller from prison

[This was printed in the *Religious Herald*, 18 January 1828. It is reproduced in Lewis Peyton Little's *Imprisoned Preachers and Religious Liberty in Virginia* (Lynchburg, Va.: J. P. Bell Co., Inc., 1938).]

Urbanna Prison, Middlesex County, August 12, 1771

Dear Brother in the Lord,

At a meeting which was held at brother McCain's, in this county, last Saturday, whilst brother William (Wm) Webber was addressing the congregation from James II.18, there came running towards him, in a most furious rage, captain James Montague, a magistrate of the county, followed by the parson of the parish, and several others who seemed greatly exasperated. The magistrate and another took hold of brother Webber, and, dragging him from the stage, delivered him, with brethren Wafford, Robert Ware, Richard Falkner, James Greenwood and myself into custody, and commanding that we should be brought before him for trial. Brother Wafford was severely scourged, and brother Henry Street received one lash, from one of the persecutors, who was prevented from proceeding to farther violence by his companions; to be short, I may inform you that we were carried before the above magistrate, who, with the parson and some others, carried us, one by one, into a room, and examined our pockets and wallets for fire-arms, &c., charging us with carrying on a mutiny against the authority of the land. Finding none, we were asked if we had license to preach in that county and learning we had not, it was required of us to give bond and security not to preach any more in the county, which we modestly refused to do, whereupon, after dismissing brother Wafford, with a charge to make his escape out of the county by twelve o'clock the next day on pain of imprisonment, and dismissing brother Falkner, the rest of us were delivered to the sheriff, and sent to close jail, with a charge not to allow us to walk in the air until court day. Blessed by God, the sheriff and jailor have treated us with as much kindness as could have been expected from strangers—may the Lord reward them for it. Yesterday we had a large number of people to hear us preach, and among others many of the great ones of the land, who behaved well while one of us discoursed on the new birth. We find the Lord gracious and kind to us beyond expression in our afflictions. We cannot tell how long we shall be kept in bonds, we therefore beseech, dear brother, that you and the church supplicate night and day for us, our benefactors, and our persecutors.

I have also to inform you that six of our brethren are confined in Caroline jail, viz: brethren Lewis Craig, John Burris, John Young, Edward Hearndon, James Goodrick and Bartholomew Cheming. The most dreadful threatenings are raised in the neighbouring counties against the Lord's faithful and humble followers. Excuse haste. Adieu,

John Waller

Charges against four Baptist preachers
in Middlesex County, 10 August 1771

[The original is in the collection of the Virginia Baptist Historical Society. This is reproduced in Lewis Peyton Little's *Imprisoned Preachers and Religious Liberty in Virginia* (Lynchburg, Va.: J. P. Bell Co., Inc., 1938).]

Middlesex ss:

James Montague one of his Majesty's Justices of the Peace of the said County

To the Sheriff or Keeper of the Gaol of the County aforesaid

I send you herewith the Bodys of John Waller, Robert Ware James Greenwood and William Webber taken this day and brought before me who stand charged with unlawfully assembling themselves at the house of James McKan in the County and taking upon them to Teach or Preach the Gospel under the pretence of the exercise of Religion in other manner than According to the Litturgy of the Church of England they not having Episcopal Ordination to Teach or Preach the same According to the Canons of the said Church of England, and not having They professing themselves to be Protestant Teachers or Preachers dissenting from the said Church of England Justified themselves as such According to the directions of and Act of the Parliament of England made in the first year of King William and Queen Mary Intitled an Act for exempting Their Majestys' Protestant Subjects dissenting from the s'd [said] Church of England from the Penalties of certain Laws, and for labouring to persuade many Persons in Communion of the Church of England to dissent from the same and for raising factions in the minds of his Majesty's Subjects contrary to the Laws of this Colony and Against the Peace of our Lord the King his Crown and Dignity:

They the said John Waller, Robert Ware, James Greenwood and William Webber, upon their trial and examination by me had and taken declare they have no Power or authority for which they stand charged, but from above, Therefore I require you to receive them into your Custody and them safely keep in the Gaol of the said County until they shall be discharged by due course of Law.

Given under my hand and Seal this 10th day of August 1771.

James Montague

Dissenters' petition to the House of Delegates, 1776

[This petition was initiated by the General Association at its meeting in Cumberland in August 1775. Although the petition was drawn up by Baptists, the goal was to secure signatures for it from as many dissenters as possible, including Presbyterians, Quakers, Mennonites, and Dunkards. When the petition was finally presented to the House of Delegates, it carried approximately ten thousand signatures. The original with the signatures may be seen in the Virginia State Library. It is reproduced in Garnett Ryland's *Baptists of Virginia: 1699-1926* (Richmond: Virginia Baptist Board of Missions and Education, 1955), pp. 99-100.]

To the Honourable the President and House of Delegates

The Petition of the Dissenters from the Ecclesiastical establishment in the Commonwealth of Virginia

Humbly sheweth

That your Petitioners being in common with the other Inhabitants of this Commonwealth delivered from British Oppression rejoice in the Prospect of having their Freedom secured and maintained to them and their posterity inviolate. The hopes of your petitioners have been raised and confirmed by the Declaration of your Honourable House with regard to equal Liberty. Equal Liberty! that invaluable blessing: which though it be the birth right of every good Member of the State has been what your Petitioners have been Deprived of, in that, by Taxation their property hath been wrested from them and given to those from whom they have received no equivalent.

Your Petitioners therefore having long groaned under the Burden of an Ecclesiastical Establishment beg leave to move your Honourable House that this as well as every other Yoke may be broken and that the Oppressed may go free: that so every religious Denomination being on a Level, Animosities may cease, and that Christian Forbearance, Love and Charity, may be practised towards each other, while the Legislature interferes only to support them in their just Rights and equal privileges.

And your Petitioners shall ever pray.

Appendix

A Memorial and Remonstrance
written by James Madison, c. 20 June 1785

[Madison had been prodded into writing his masterpiece on church-state relations by George Nicholas and his brother Wilson Cary Nicholas. However, the public at large was unaware that Madison was the author of the memorial. It was circulated in thirteen or more petitions and garnered 1,552 signatures. Another anonymous petition, called "the formula petition," by Thomas Buckley (author of *Church and State in Revolutionary Virginia: 1776-1787*) was initiated by the General Committee in August 1785. This petition, launched in opposition to the General Assessment Bill, was based upon a theological principle that held it "repugnant to the spirit of the gospel for the legislature thus to proceed in matters of religion." It was circulated in twenty-nine separate petitions and garnered 4,899 signatures. Other petitions were also prepared and promoted among the general public. As Garnett Ryland indicates, "It was the policy of the Baptists to prepare and promote petitions signed by citizens generally" (*The Baptists of Virginia: 1699-1926* [Richmond: Virginia Baptist Board of Missions and Education, 1955], p. 125). The original is found in the Library of Congress. It is reproduced in *The Papers of James Madison*, vol. 8, ed. Robert A. Rutland and William M. E. Rachal (Chicago: University of Chicago Press, 1973), pp. 298-304.]

To the Honorable the General Assembly of the Commonwealth of Virginia:

A Memorial and Remonstrance

We the subscribers, citizens of the said Commonwealth, having taken into serious consideration, a Bill printed by order of the last Session of General Assembly, entitled "A Bill establishing a provision for Teachers of the Christian Religion," and conceiving that the same if finally armed with the sanctions of a law, will be a dangerous abuse of power, are bound as faithful members of a free State to remonstrate against it, and to declare the reasons by which we are determined. We remonstrate against the said Bill,

    1. Because we hold it for a fundamental and undeniable

185

truth, "that Religion or the duty which we owe to our Creator and the manner of discharging it, can be directed only by reason and conviction, not by force or violence." The Religion then of every man must be left to the conviction and conscience of every man; and it is the right of every man to exercise it as these may dictate. This right is in its nature an unalienable right. It is unalienable, because the opinions of men, depending only on the evidence contemplated by their own minds cannot follow the dictates of other men: It is unalienable also, because what is here a right towards men, is a duty towards the Creator. It is the duty of every man to render to the Creator such homage and such only as he believes to be acceptable to him. This duty is precedent, both in order of time and in degree of obligation, to the claims of Civil Society. Before any man can be considered as a member of Civil Society, he must be considered as a subject of the Governour of the Universe: And if a member of Civil Society, who enters into any subordinate Association, must always do it with a reservation of his duty to the General Authority; much more must every man who becomes a member of any particular Civil Society, do it with a saving of his allegiance to the Universal Sovereign. We maintain therefore that in matters of Religion, no mans right is abridged by the institution of Civil Society and that Religion is wholly exempt from its cognizance. True it is, that no other rule exists, by which any question which may divide a Society, can be ultimately determined, but the will of the majority; but it is also true that the majority may trespass on the rights of the minority.

2. Because if Religion be exempt from the authority of the Society at large, still less can it be subject to that of the Legislative Body. The latter are but the creatures and vicegerents of the former. Their jurisdiction is both derivative and limited: it is limited with regard to the co-ordinate departments, more necessarily is it limited with regard to the constituents. The preservation of a free Government requires not merely, that the metes and bounds which separate each department of power be invariably maintained; but more especially that neither of them be suffered to overleap the great Barrier which defends the rights of the people. The Rulers who are guilty of such an encroach-

ment, exceed the commission from which they derive their authority, and are Tyrants. The People who submit to it are governed by laws made neither by themselves nor by an authority derived from them, and are slaves.

3. Because it is proper to take alarm at the first experiment on our liberties. We hold this prudent jealousy to be the first duty of Citizens, and one of the noblest characteristics of the late Revolution. The free men of America did not wait till usurped power had strengthened itself by exercise, and entangled the question in precedents. They saw all the consequences in the principle, and they avoided the consequences by denying the principle. We revere this lesson too much soon to forget it. Who does not see that the same authority which can establish Christianity, in exclusion of all other Religions, may establish with the same ease any particular sect of Christians, in exclusion of all other Sects? that the same authority which can force a citizen to contribute three pence only of his property for the support of any one establishment, may force him to conform to any other establishment in all cases whatsoever?

4. Because the Bill violates that equality which ought to be the basis of every law, and which is more indispensable, in proportion as the validity or expediency of any law is more liable to be impeached. If "all men are by nature equally free and independent," all men are to be considered as entering into Society on equal conditions; as relinquishing no more, and therefore retaining no less, one than another, of their natural rights. Above all are they to be considered as retaining an "*equal title to the free exercise of Religion according to the dictates of Conscience.*" Whilst we assert for ourselves a freedom to embrace, to profess and to observe the Religion which we believe to be of divine origin, we cannot deny an equal freedom to those whose minds have not yet yielded to the evidence which has convinced us. If this freedom be abused, it is an offence against God, not against man: To God, therefore, not to man, must an account of it be rendered. As the Bill violates equality by subjecting some peculiar burdens, so it violates the same principle, by granting to others peculiar exemptions. Are the

Quakers and Menonists the only sects who think a compulsive support of their Religions unnecessary and unwarrantable? Can their piety alone be entrusted with the care of public worship? Ought their Religions to be endowed above all others with extraordinary privileges by which proselytes may be enticed from all others? We think too favorable of the justice and good sense of these denominations to believe that they either covet pre-eminences over their fellow citizens or that they will be seduced by them from the common opposition to the measure.

5. Because the Bill implies either that the Civil Magistrate is a competent Judge of Religious Truth; or that he may employ Religion as an engine of Civil policy. The first is an arrogant pretension falsified by the contradictory opinions of Rulers in all ages, and throughout the world: the second an unhallowed perversion of the means of salvation.

6. Because the establishment proposed by the Bill is not requisite for the support of the Christian Religion. To say that it is, is a contradiction to the Christian Religion itself, for every page of it disavows a dependence on the powers of this world: it is a contradiction to fact; for it is known that this Religion both existed and flourished, not only without the support of human laws, but in spite of every opposition from them, and not only during the period of miraculous aid, but long after it had been left to its own evidence and the ordinary care of Providence. Nay, it is a contradiction in terms; for a Religion not invented by human policy, must have pre-existed and been supported, before it was established by human policy. It is moreover to weaken in those who profess this Religion a pious confidence in its innate excellence and the patronage of its Author; and to foster in those who still reject it, a suspicion that its friends are too conscious of its fallacies to trust its own merits.

7. Because experience witnesseth that ecclesiastical establishments, instead of maintaining the purity and efficacy of Religion, have had a contrary operation. During almost fifteen centuries has the legal establishment of Christianity been on trial. What have been its fruits? More or less in all places, pride and indolence in the Clergy, ignorance and servility in the laity, in both, superstition, bigotry and persecution. Enquire of the

Teachers of Christianity for the ages in which it appeared in its greatest lustre; those of every sect, point to the ages prior to its incorporation with Civil policy. Propose a restoration of this primitive State in which its Teachers depended on the voluntary rewards of their flocks, many of them predict its downfall. On which Side ought their testimony to have greatest weight, when for or when against their interest?

8. Because of the establishment in question is not necessary for the support of Civil government. If it be urged as necessary for the support of Civil Government only as it is a means of supporting Religion, and it be not necessary for the latter purpose, it cannot be necessary for the former. If Religion be not within the cognizance of Civil Government how can its legal establishment be necessary to Civil Government? What influence in fact have ecclesiastical establishments had on Civil Society? In some instances they have been seen to erect a spiritual tyranny on the ruins of the Civil authority; in many instances they have been seen upholding the thrones of political tyranny; in no instance have they been seen the guardians of the liberties of the people. Rulers who wished to subvert the public liberty, may have found an established Clergy convenient auxiliaries. A just Government instituted to secure & perpetuate it needs them not. Such a Government will be best supported by protecting every Citizen in the enjoyment of his Religion with the same equal hand which protects his person and his property; by neither invading the equal rights of any Sect, nor suffering any Sect to invade those of another.

9. Because the proposed establishment is a departure from that generous policy, which, offering an Asylum to the persecuted and oppressed of every Nation and Religion, promised a lustre to our country, and an accession to the number of its citizens. What a melancholy mark is the Bill of sudden degeneracy? Instead of holding forth an Asylum to the persecuted, it is itself a signal of persecution. It degrades from the equal rank of Citizen all those whose opinions in Religion do not bend to those of the Legislative authority. Distant as it may be in its present form from the Inquisition, it differs from it only in degree. The one is the first step, the other the last in the career

of intolerance. The magnanimous sufferer under this cruel scourge in foreign Regions, must view the Bill as a Beacon on our Coast, warning him to seek some other haven, where liberty and philanthropy in their due extent, may offer a more certain repose from his Troubles.

10. Because it will have a like tendency to banish our Citizens. The allurements presented by other situations are every day thinning their number. To superadd a fresh motive to emigration by revoking the liberty which they now enjoy, would be the same species of folly which has dishonoured and depopulated flourishing kingdoms.

11. Because it will destroy that moderation and harmony which the forbearance of our laws to intermeddle with Religion has produced among its several sects. Torrents of blood have been spilt in the old world, by vain attempts of the secular arm, to extinguish Religious discord, by proscribing all difference in Religious opinion. Time has at length revealed the true remedy. Every relaxation of narrow and rigorous policy, wherever it has been tried, has been found to assuage the disease. The American Theatre has exhibited proofs that equal and compleat liberty, if it does not wholly eradicate it, sufficiently destroys its malignant influence on the health and prosperity of the State. If with the salutary effects of this system under our own eyes, we begin to contract the bounds of Religious freedom, we know no name that will too severely reproach our folly. At least let warning be taken at the first fruits of the threatened innovation. The very appearance of the Bill has transformed "that Christian forbearance, love and charity," which of late mutually prevailed, into animosities and jealousies, which may not soon be appeased. What mischiefs may not be dreaded, should this enemy to the public quiet be armed with the force of a law?

12. Because the policy of the Bill is adverse to the diffusion of the light of Christianity. The first wish of those who enjoy this precious gift ought to be that it may be imparted to the whole race of mankind. Compare the number of those who have as yet received it with the number still remaining under the dominion of false Religions; and how small is the former! Does the policy of the Bill tend to lessen the disproportion? No; it at

190

once discourages those who are strangers to the light of revelation from coming into the Region of it; and countenances by example the nations who continue in darkness, in shutting out those who might convey it to them. Instead of Levelling as far as possible, every obstacle to the victorious progress of Truth, the Bill with an ignoble and unchristian timidity would circumscribe it with a wall of defense against the encroachments of error.

13. Because attempts to enforce by legal sanctions, acts obnoxious to so great a proportion of Citizens, tend to enervate the laws in general, and to slacken the bands of Society. If it be difficult to execute any law which is not generally deemed necessary or salutary, what must be the case, where it is deemed invalid and dangerous? and what may be the effect of so striking an example of impotency in the government, on its general authority?

14. Because a measure of such singular magnitude and delicacy ought not to be imposed, without the clearest evidence that it is called for by a majority of citizens, and no satisfactory method is yet proposed by which the voice of the majority in this case may be determined, or its influence secured. "The people of the respective counties are indeed requested to signify their opinion respecting the adoption of the Bill to the next Session of Assembly." But the representation must be made equal, before the voice of either of the Representatives or of the Counties will be that of the people. Our hope is that neither of the former will, after due consideration, espouse the dangerous principle of the Bill. Should the event disappoint us, it will still leave us in full confidence, that a fair appeal to the latter will reverse the sentence against our liberties.

15. Because finally, "the equal right of every citizen to the free exercise of his Religion according to the dictates of conscience" is held by the same tenure with all our other rights. If we recur to its origin, it is equally the gift of nature; if we weigh its importance, it cannot be less dear to us; if we consult the "Declaration of those rights which pertain to the good people of Virginia, as the basis and foundation of Government," it is enumerated with equal solemnity, or rather studied emphasis.

Either then, we must say, that the Will of the Legislature is the only measure of their authority; and that in the plenitude of this authority, they may sweep away all our fundamental rights; or, that they are bound to leave this particular right untouched and sacred: Either we must say, that they may controul the freedom of the press, may abolish the Trial by Jury, may swallow up the Executive and Judiciary Powers of the State; nay that they may despoil us of our very right of suffrage, and erect themselves into an independent and hereditary Assembly or, we must say, that they have no authority to enact into law the Bill under consideration. We the Subscribers say, that the General Assembly of this Commonwealth have no such authority: And that no effort may be omitted on our part against so dangerous an usurpation, we oppose to it, this remonstrance; earnestly praying, as we are in duty bound, that the Supreme Lawgiver of the Universe, by illuminating those to whom it is addressed, may on the one hand, turn their Councils from the very act which would affront his holy prerogative, or violate the trust committed to them: and on the other, guide them into every measure which may be worthy of his [blessing, may re]dound to their own praise, and may establish more firmly the liberties, the prosperity and the happiness of the Commonwealth.

Petition against the General Assessment Bill formulated and circulated by the General Committee, August 1785

[The original petitions are in the Virginia State Library. They are reproduced in Garnett Ryland's *Baptists of Virginia: 1699-1926* (Richmond: Virginia Baptist Board of Missions and Education, 1955), pp. 124-25.]

That it be recommended to those counties, which have not yet prepared petitions to be presented to the General Assembly against the engrossed bill for a general assessment for the support of the teachers of the Christian religion, to proceed thereon as soon as possible: That it is believed to be repugnant to the spirit of the gospel for the legislature thus to proceed in matters of religion; that the holy author of our religion needs no such compulsive measures for the promotion of his cause; that the gospel wants not the feeble arm of man for its support; that it has made and will again through divine power make its way against all opposition; and that should the legislature assume the right of taxing the people for the support of the gospel it will be destructive to religious liberty.

"An Act for Establishing Religious Freedom" by Thomas Jefferson, 1786

[Jefferson wrote this statute in 1777. Two years later, in 1779, it was introduced to the House of Delegates, where it did not receive the necessary third reading and consequently was tabled. Resurrected at an opportune time by James Madison, it passed into law with only slight revisions made to the original version. The original is housed in the Virginia State Library. It is reproduced in *The Papers of Thomas Jefferson*, vol. 2, ed. Julian P. Boyd (Princeton: Princeton University Press, 1950), pp. 545-47.]

An Act for Establishing Religious Freedom

I. Whereas Almighty God hath created the mind free; that all attempts to influence it by temporal punishments or burthens, or by civil incapacitations, tend only to beget habits of hypocrisy and meanness, and are a departure from the plan of the Holy author of our religion, who being Lord both of body and mind, yet chose not to propagate it by coercions on either, as was in his Almighty power to do; that the impious presumption of legislators and rulers, civil as well as ecclesiastical, who being themselves but fallible and uninspired men, have assumed dominion over the faith of others, setting up their own opinions and modes of thinking as the only true and infallible, and as such endeavouring to impose them on others, hath established and maintained false religions over the greatest part of the world, and through all time; that to compel a man to furnish contributions of money for the propagation of opinions which he disbelieves, is sinful and tyrannical; that even the forcing [of] him to support this or that teacher of his own religious persuasion, is depriving him of the comfortable liberty of giving his contributions to the particular pastor, whose morals he would make his pattern, and whose powers he feels most persuasive to righteousness, and is withdrawing from the ministry those temporary rewards, which proceeding from an approbation of their personal conduct, are an additional incitement to earnest and unremitting labours for the instruction of mankind; that our civil rights have no dependence on our religious opinions, any more than our opinions in physics or geometry; that therefore the proscribing [of] any citizen as unworthy [of] the public confidence by laying upon him an incapacity of being called to offices of trust and emolument, unless he profess or renounce this or that religious opinion, is depriving him injuriously of those privileges and advantages to which in common with his fellow-citizens he has a natural right; that it tends only to corrupt the principles of that religion it is meant to encourage, by bribing with a monopoly of worldly honours and emoluments, those who will externally profess and conform to it; that though indeed these are criminal who do not withstand such temptation, yet neither are those innocent who lay the bait in their way; that to suffer the civil magistrate to intrude his powers into the field of opinion, and to restrain the profession or propagation of principles on supposition of their ill tendency, is a dangerous fallacy, which at once destroys all religious liberty, because he being of course judge of that tendency will make his opinions the rule of judgment; and approve or condemn the sentiments of others only as they shall square with or differ from his own; that it is time enough for the rightful purposes of civil government, for its officers to interfere when principles break out into overt acts against peace and good order; and finally, that truth is great and will prevail if left to herself, that she is the proper and sufficient antagonist to error, and has nothing to fear from the conflict, unless by human interposition disarmed of her natural weapons, free argument and debate, errors ceasing to be dangerous when it is permitted freely to contradict them:

II. *Be it enacted by the General Assembly,* That no man shall be compelled to frequent or support any religious worship, place, or ministry whatsoever, nor shall be enforced, restrained, molested, or burthened in his body or goods, nor shall otherwise suffer on account of his religious opinions or belief; but that all men shall be free to profess, and by argument to maintain, their opinion in matters of religion, and that the same shall in no wise diminish, enlarge, or affect their civil capacities.

The memorial of the General Committee to the General Assembly for the repeal of the Incorporation Act, 5 August 1786

[The original is in the Virginia State Library. It is reproduced in Garnett Ryland's *Baptists of Virginia: 1699-1926* (Richmond: Virginia Baptist Board of Missions and Education, 1955), pp. 127-30.]

The Representatives of Several Baptist Associations in Virginia Assembled in Committee, August 5, 1786, Beg leave Respectfully to address your Honorable House:

When Britain, with her cruel Usurpation over her Colonies in America, reduced them to the necessity of taking up Arms to vindicate their Natural Claims, A declaration of Rights was made by the good People of Virginia, Assembled in full and free Convention, as the Basis and foundation of Government and A Constitution, so Liberal in Civil and free in religious concerns, that we readily took the Oath of Fidelity to the State. From this principle we expatiated! for this free government we advanced our property and exposed our lives on the field of battle with our fellow Citizens; being often Stimulated with the harmonious Proclamation of equal Liberty of conscience and equal claim of property.

As hazardous as the Enterprise appeared: under the interposition of divine providence, by the prudence of our Ambassadors, the wisdom of our politicians, the skill of our Generals, the bravery of our soldiers and the aid of our Allies, after a seven years Contest we obtained our liberty and Independence with a vast empire added to us by the late treaty of peace. At this happy period, when America emerged from a bloody Obscurity to such a distinguishing figure of importance among the nations of the world: we felicitated our Selves with the enjoyment of every domestic and Social blessing of human Life. Nor were we willing to harbour a jealous thought of the Legislature, that the Bill of Rights would not be attended to in every particular.

But, to our great Surprize, in the Session of 1784, at the request of a few Clergymen, the members of the late established Church of England were incorporated into a Society, called the "Protestant Episcopal Church," as a body Corporate and politic. To the ministers and members of that Church and their Successors were given all and every Tract, or Tracts, of Glebe Land already purchased, and every other thing the property of the late established Church of England, to the Sole and only use of the Protestant Episcopal Church. If Religion or the duty which we owe to our Creator, and the manner of discharging it, can be directed only by reason and conviction, not by force and violence (so fully expressed in the XVI Art. of the Bill of Rights, and the late Act for establishing Religious Liberty) we cannot see with what propriety the General Assembly could incorporate the Protestant Episcopal Church, give her a name, Describe the character of her members, modulate the forms of her government & appoint the Time and place of her meeting. If this is not done by force, what force can there be in law? and to what lengths this may lead and what violence it may produce, time only can discover, but we fear the awful consequences. The act appears a Bitumen to Cement Church and State together: the foundation for Ecclesiastical Tyranny and the first steps towards an Inquisition.

New Testament Churches, we humbly conceive, are, or should be, established by the Legislature of Heaven and not earthly power; by the Law of God and not the Law of the State; by the acts of the Apostles and not by the Acts of an Assembly. The Incorporating Act, then, in the first place, appears to cast great contempt upon the divine Author of our Religion, whose Kingdom is not of this world. Secondly, to give all the property of the State established church to one Society, not more virtuous or deserving than other Societies in the commonwealth, appears contrary to justice and the express words of the IV Art. of the Bill of Rights, which prohibits rewards or emoluments to any Man, or set of men, except for services rendered the State; and what services that Church has rendered the State, either by her Clergy or Laity, more than other Churches have done, we know not.

If truth is great, and will prevail if left to itself (as declared in the Act Establishing Religious Freedom) we wish it may be so left, which is the only way to convince the gazing world that Disciples do not follow Christ for Loaves, and that Preachers do not preach for Benefices.

From the days of Edward the VI, when the Liturgy was first framed, to the year 1661 it was at several times changed and revised by publick authority. This at once shows the fickleness of human Establishments, and while things are so mutable it appears dangerous to religious Liberty for the legislature to establish Rules and Directions for the Church, unless we were assured our Consciences and Sentiments would always acquiesce in the will of the Legislature.

It is well known that Ecclesiastical Establishment is one part of the British Constitution, and, therefore, the Church of England is obliged to own the King of Great Britain to be her Head. Our declaration of Independence appears to have made every Son of Liberty in America a Dissenter from that Church; but if that does not completely do it, has not the Protestant Episcopal Church since done it in disapproving of a number of old Articles, and forms of worship? If Dissenters, therefore, have no right to that Property it seems That Church cannot lay a just claim to it.

If the members of the Protestant Episcopal Church prefer Episcopacy to any other form of Government, they have an undoubted Right as free Citizens of the State to enjoy it. But to call in the aid of Legislature to Establish it threatens the freedom of Religious Liberty in its Consequences. And, whereas, the Incorporating Act appears to be pregnant with evil and dangerous to religious Liberty, your Petitioners humbly remonstrate against it; and trust that the wisdom of your Hon. House will repeal the exceptionable parts of the said Act and apply the property to the use of the community in such a manner as [to] you shall seem just.

William Webber, Clk.

"John Leland's Objections to the Constitution without a Bill of Rights," sent to James Madison by Joseph Spencer, 28 February 1788

[Leland shared his objections personally with James Madison on the eve of Madison's election as a delegate from Orange County to the ratifying convention. Apparently Leland and Madison became staunch friends, a development implied by subsequent correspondence between them. Leland's major concern was the lack of sufficient guarantees for religious liberty in the federal Constitution. In this he expressed the concerns of the General Committee and other dissenters as well. The original copy of Leland's objections is in the Madison Papers housed in the Library of Congress. Contrary to what one would expect, the objections are not in *The Papers of James Madison*, ed. Robert A. Rutland and William M. E. Rachal (Chicago: University of Chicago Press, 1973), although there is an extended footnote referring to them in volume 11 (p. 541). However, the objections are reproduced in L. H. Butterfield's *Elder John Leland, Jeffersonian Itinerant* (New York: Arno Press, 1980), pp. 187-90.]

Sir

According to your Request, I have sent you my objections to the *Federal Constitution*, which are as follows:

1st. There is no Bill of Rights, whenever a Number of men enter into a state of Society, a Number of individual Rights must be given up to Society, but there should be a memorial of those not surrendered, otherwise every natural & domestic Right becomes alianable, which raises Tyranny at once, and this is as necessary in one Form of Government as in another.

2nd. There is a Contradiction in the Constitution, we are first inform'd that all Legislative Powers therein granted shall be Vested in a Congress composed of *two houses*, and yet afterwards all the power that lies between a majority and two thirds, which is one Sixth part, is taken from these *two Houses*, and given to one man, who is not only chosen two Removes from the people, but also the head of the executive Department.

3rd. The House of Representatives is the only free, direct

Representation of the body of the people, and yet in Treaties which are to be some of the Supreme Laws of the Land, this House has no voice.

4th. The Time place and Manner of chusing the members of the Lower house is intirely at the Mercy of Congress, if they Appoint Pipin or Japan, or their ten Miles Square for the place, no man can help it. How can Congress guarantee to each State a Republican form of government, when every principle of Republicanism is sapped.

5th. The Senators are chosen for Six years, and when they are once Chosen, they are impeachable to nun but themselves, No Counterprize is left in the hands of the People, or even in Legislative Bodys to check them, Vote as they will, there they set, paying themselves at Pleasure.

6th. I utterly oppose any Division in a Legislative Body, the more Houses, the more parties, the more they are Divided, the more the Wisdom is Scattered, sometimes one house may prevent the error of another and the same stands true of twenty Houses. But the question is, whether they do more good than harm, the Business is certainly thereby retarded and the Expence inhanced.

7th. We are not informed whether Votes in all cases in the Lower house are to be by Members or by States,—I Question whether a man could find out the Riddle by plowing, with Sampsons Heifers, if each Member is not to have a Vote, why are they to be chosen according to Numbers of Inhabitants, and why should Virginia be at ten times the Expense of Delaware for the same Powers, if the Votes are always to be by States, why is it not Expressed as in the choice of a President, in certain cases, If each Member is to have a Vote Why is it Expressed concerning Senators, and not concerning Representatives, this Blank appears to be designed, to encourage the Small States with hopes of Equality, and the Large States with hopes of Superiority.

8ly. We have no asurance that the Liberty of the press will be allowed under this Constitution.

9ly. We have always been taught that it was dangerous mixing the Legislative and Executive Powers together in the same body of People, but in this Constitution we are taught better, or worse.

10ly. What is clearest of all—Religious Liberty, is not sufficiently secured, No Religious test is Required as a qualification to fill any office under the United States, but if a Majority of Congress with the President favour one System more then another, they may oblige all others to pay to the support of their System as much as they please, and if Oppression does not ensue, it will be owing to the Mildness of Administration and not to any Constitutional defence, and if the Manners of People are so far Corrupted, that they cannot live by Republican principles, it is Very Dangerous leaving Religious Liberty at their Mercy.

Revd. John Leeland's Objections to the Federal Constitution Sent to Colo. Thos. Barber by his Request, a Coppy taken by Jos. Spencer entended for the Consideration of Capt. Jas. Walker Culpeper.

Selected Bibliography

Abbott, Walter M., and Joseph Gallagher, eds. *The Documents of Vatican II.* New York: Guild Press, 1966.

Alley, Reuben Edward. *A History of Baptists in Virginia.* Richmond: Virginia Baptist General Board, 1973.

Backus, Isaac. *A History of New England with Particular Reference to the Denomination of Christians Called Baptists.* 2nd ed. 2 vols. Newton, Mass.: Backus Historical Society, 1871.

————. *Isaac Backus on Church, State, and Calvinism: Pamphlets, 1754-1789.* Ed. William G. McLoughlin. Cambridge: Belknap Press, 1968.

Bainton, Roland H. *The Travail of Religious Liberty.* New York: Harper & Brothers, 1951.

Bergsten, Torsten. *Balthasar Hubmaier.* Trans. Irwin J. Barnes and William R. Estep. Ed. William R. Estep. Valley Forge, Pa.: Judson Press, 1978.

Bicknell, Thomas W. *Story of Dr. John Clarke.* Providence, R.I.: n.p., 1915.

Bradford, William. *Of Plymouth Plantation.* Ed. Harvey Wish. New York: Capricorn Books, 1962.

Buckley, Thomas E. *Church and State in Revolutionary Virginia: 1776-1787.* Charlottesville, Va.: University Press of Virginia, 1977.

Burrage, Champlin. *The Early English Dissenters in the Light of Recent Research (1550-1641).* 2 vols. 1912; repr. New York: Russell & Russell, 1967.

Butterfield, L. H. *Elder John Leland, Jeffersonian Itinerant.* New York: Arno Press, 1980.

Callender, John. *The Early History of Rhode Island.* Ed. Romeo Elton. Freeport, N.Y.: Books for Libraries Press, 1843.

Coggins, James Robert. "John Smyth's Congregation: English Separatism, Dutch Mennonites and the Elect Nation." Ph.D. diss., University of Waterloo, 1987.

Colson, Charles. *The Role of the Church in Society.* Wheaton, Ill.: Victor Books, 1986.

"A Confession of Faith of Seven Congregations or Churches of Christ in London, which are Commonly (but unjustly) Called Anabaptists." 1646; repr. Rochester, N.Y.: Backus Book Publishers, 1981.

Cotton, John. "A Discourse about Civil Government." In *Church and State in American History: The Burden of Religious Pluralism.* 2nd ed. Ed. John F. Wilson and Donald L. Drakeman. Boston: Beacon Press, 1987.

Creed, J. Bradley. "American Prophet of Religious Individualism." Ph.D. diss., Southwestern Baptist Theological Seminary, 1986.

Crosby, Thomas. *The History of the English Baptists, from the Reformation to the Beginning of the Reign of King George I.* 4 vols. 1738; repr. Lafayette, Tenn.: Church History Research & Archives, 1979.

Cunningham, Noble E., Jr. *In Pursuit of Reason: The Life of Thomas Jefferson.* Baton Rouge: Louisiana State University Press, 1987.

Dawson, Joseph Martin. *Baptists and the American Republic.* Nashville: Broadman Press, 1956.

DeJong, Norman. "Separation of Church and State: Historical Reality or Judicial Myth?" *Fides et Historia* 18 (Jan. 1986): 25-37.

Edwards, Jonathan. *The Works of Jonathan Edwards,* vol. 4: *The Great Awakening.* Ed. C. C. Goen. New Haven: Yale University Press, 1972.

Eidsmoe, John. *God and Caesar: Christian Faith and Political Action.* Westchester, Ill.: Crossway Books, 1984.

Ernst, James. *Roger Williams, New England Firebrand.* New York: Macmillan, 1932.

Finlator, W. W. "They're Trying to Make Us Baptists!" *Christian Century,* 6 Apr. 1983, p. 303.

Fox, Steve. "Why SBC Right Upset with Dunn and Baptist Joint Committee." *SBC Today,* Jan. 1989, p. 20.

Fremantle, Anne, ed. *The Papal Encyclicals in Their Historical Context.* New York: New American Library, 1963.

Garrison, W. E. "Characteristics of American Organized Religion." *Annals of the American Academy of Political and Social Science* 256 (March 1948): 17.

Gaustad, Edwin S. *Baptist Piety*. Grand Rapids: Wm. B. Eerdmans, 1978.

————. *Faith of Our Fathers: Religion and the New Nation*. San Francisco: Harper & Row, 1987.

————. *A Religious History of America*. New York: Harper & Row, 1966.

————, ed. *Colonial Baptists and Southern Revivals*. New York: Arno Press, 1980.

Gilpin, W. Clark. *The Millenarian Piety of Roger Williams*. Chicago: University of Chicago Press, 1979.

Gleeson, Alice Collins. *Colonial Rhode Island*. Pawtucket, R.I.: Automobile Journal Publishing Co., 1926.

Grenz, Stanley. *Isaac Backus: Puritan and Baptist*. Macon, Ga.: Mercer University Press, 1983.

Gritz, Paul Linton. "Samuel Richardson and the Religious and Political Controversies Confronting the London Particular Baptists, 1643 to 1658." Ph.D. diss., Southwestern Baptist Theological Seminary, 1987.

Haller, William. *The Rise of Puritanism*. New York: Harper & Row, 1957.

Hamilton, Alexander, et al. *Selections from The Federalist: A Commentary on the Constitution of the United States*. Ed. Henry S. Commager. Arlington Heights, Ill.: Harlan Davidson, Inc., 1949.

Hauben, Paul J. *The Spanish Inquisition*. New York: John Wiley & Sons, 1969.

Helwys, Thomas. *The Mistery of Iniquity*. Oxford: Bodleian Library; repr. London: Kingsgate Press, 1935.

Holmes, Obadiah. *Baptist Piety: The Last Will and Testimony of Obadiah Holmes*. Ed. Edwin S. Gaustad. Grand Rapids: Wm. B. Eerdmans, 1978.

Horst, Irvin B. *Radical Brethren: Anabaptism and the English Reformation to 1558*. Nieuwkoop: De Graaf, 1972.

Howell, John N. "Northern-Jeffersonian–Republican Ministers and the Election of 1800." Unpublished paper. Alexandria, Va., 1988.

Hubmaier, Balthasar. *Balthasar Hubmaier Schriften*. Ed. Gunnar Westin and Torsten Bergsten. Heidelberg: Verein für Reformationsgeschichte, 1962.

Hudson, Winthrop. *Religion in America*. New York: Macmillan, 1987.

Isaac, Rhys. *The Transformation of Virginia: 1740-1790*. Chapel Hill: University of North Carolina Press, 1982.

James, Joseph B. *The Framing of the Fourteenth Amendment*. Urbana: University of Illinois Press, 1965.

Jefferson, Thomas. *Basic Writings of Thomas Jefferson.* Ed. Philip S. Foner. New York: Wiley Book Co., 1944.

———. *Notes on Virginia.* In vol. 2 of *The Writings of Thomas Jefferson.* Ed. Albert Ellery Bergh. Washington: Thomas Jefferson Memorial Association of the United States, 1905.

———. *The Papers of Thomas Jefferson.* Ed. Julian P. Boyd et al. 22 vols. Princeton: Princeton University Press, 1950–.

Kenyon, J. P. *The Stuarts: A Study of English Kingship.* London: Collins-Fontana, 1958.

Köhler, Walther, and Harold S. Bender. "Martin Luther." In *The Mennonite Encyclopedia,* vol. 3. Scottdale, Pa.: Mennonite Publishing House, 1957, pp. 416-22.

Leland, John. *The Writings of John Leland.* Ed. L. F. Greene. New York: Arno Press & the *New York Times,* 1969.

Levy, Leonard W. *The Establishment Clause.* New York: Macmillan, 1986.

Littell, Franklin Hamlin. *From State Church to Pluralism: A Protestant Interpretation of Religion in American History.* Garden City, N.Y.: Doubleday-Anchor Books, 1962.

Little, Lewis Peyton. *Imprisoned Preachers and Religious Liberty in Virginia.* Lynchburg, Va.: J. P. Bell Co., Inc., 1938.

Lumpkin, William L. *Baptist Confessions of Faith.* Philadelphia: Judson Press, 1959.

———. *Baptist Foundations in the South.* Nashville: Broadman Press, 1961.

MacMaster, Richard K., Samuel L. Horst, and Robert F. Ulle. *Conscience in Crisis.* Scottdale, Pa.: Herald Press, 1979.

Madison, James. *The Papers of James Madison.* Vol. 8. Ed. Robert A. Rutland and William M. E. Rachal. Chicago: University of Chicago Press, 1973.

Marsden, George. *Fundamentalism and American Culture: The Shaping of Twentieth-Century Evangelicalism.* New York: Oxford University Press, 1980.

Maston, T. B. *Pioneer of Religious Liberty.* Rochester, N.Y.: American Baptist Historical Society, 1962.

Mead, Sidney. *The Lively Experiment.* New York: Harper & Row, 1963.

Menendez, Albert J. *Religion at the Polls.* Philadelphia: Westminster Press, 1977.

Miller, Glenn T. *Religious Liberty in America: History and Prospects.* Philadelphia: Westminster Press, 1976.

Miller, Perry. *Roger Williams: His Contribution to the American Tradition.* New York: Atheneum, 1962.

Miller, William Lee. *The First Liberty: Religion and the American Republic.* New York: Alfred A. Knopf, 1985.

Nelson, Wilbur. *The Hero of Aquidneck: A Life of Dr. John Clarke.* 1938; repr. Bloomfield, N.J.: Schaefer Enterprises, 1954.

Neuhaus, Richard John. *The Naked Public Square.* Grand Rapids: Wm. B. Eerdmans, 1984.

Newman, A. H. *A History of the Baptist Churches in the United States.* New York: Christian Literature Co., 1894.

———. *A Manual of Church History.* 2 vols. Philadelphia: American Baptist Publication Society, 1931.

North, Gary. "Tactics of Christian Resistance." In *Christianity and Civilization.* Ed. James B. Jordan and Gary North. Tyler, Tex.: Geneva Divinity School, 1983.

Pfeffer, Leo. *Church, State, and Freedom.* Boston: Beacon Press, 1953.

Pierard, Richard V. *Bibliography on the New Christian Right.* Terre Haute, Ind.: Richard V. Pierard, 1981.

———. "Religion and the 1984 Election Campaign." *Review of Religious Research* 27 (Dec. 1985).

Renwick, A. M. *The Story of the Scottish Reformation.* Grand Rapids: Wm. B. Eerdmans, 1960.

Robinson, John. *The Works of John Robinson, Pastor of the Pilgrim Fathers.* Ed. Robert Ashton. 3 vols. London: John Snow, 1851.

Rutland, Robert Allen. *The Birth of the Bill of Rights, 1776-1791.* Chapel Hill: University of North Carolina Press, 1955.

Ryland, Garnett. *The Baptists of Virginia: 1699-1926.* Richmond: Virginia Baptist Board of Missions and Education, 1955.

Semple, Robert Baylor. *History of the Baptists in Virginia.* First published in 1810, revised and extended by G. W. Beale. Lafayette, Tenn.: Church History Research and Archives, 1976.

Shurden, Walter B., ed. *The Life of Baptists in the Life of the World.* Nashville: Broadman Press, 1985.

Simons, Menno. *The Complete Writings of Menno Simons, c. 1496-1561.* Trans. Leonard Verduin. Ed. John Christian Wenger. Scottdale, Pa.: Herald Press, 1956.

Smith, Shelton H., Robert T. Handy, and Lefferts A. Loetscher, eds. *American Christianity: An Historical Interpretation with Representative Documents.* 2 vols. New York: Charles Scribner's Sons, 1960.

Smyth, John. *The Works of John Smyth, Fellow of Christ's College, 1594-1598.* Ed. W. T. Whitley. 2 vols. Cambridge: Cambridge University Press, 1915.

Sprunger, Keith L. *Dutch Puritanism*. Vol. 31 of Studies on the History of Christian Thought. Atlantic Highlands, N.J.: Humanities Press, 1982.

Sweet, William Warren. *The Story of Religion in America*. New York: Harper & Row, 1950.

Underhill, Edward Bean, ed. *Tracts on Liberty of Conscience and Persecution: 1614-1661*. London: Hanserd Knollys Society, 1846.

Underwood, A. C. *A History of the English Baptists*. London: Carey Kingsgate Press Limited, 1947.

Verduin, Leonard. *The Anatomy of a Hybrid: A Study in Church-State Relationships*. Grand Rapids: Wm. B. Eerdmans, 1976.

———. *The Reformers and Their Stepchildren*. Grand Rapids: Wm. B. Eerdmans, 1964.

Watts, Michael R. *The Dissenters*, vol. 1: *From the Reformation to the French Revolution*. Oxford: Clarendon Press, 1978.

Williams, Glanmor. *Reformation Views of Church History*. Ed. Martin Marty et al. No. 11 in Ecumenical Studies in History series. London: Lutterworth Press, 1970.

Williams, Roger. *The Complete Writings of Roger Williams*. Ed. Samuel L. Caldwell and J. Lewis Diman. 7 vols. New York: Russell & Russell, 1963.

———. "Queries of Highest Considerations." In *Church and State in American History: The Burden of Religious Pluralism*. 2nd ed. Ed. John F. Wilson and Donald Drakeman. Boston: Beacon Press, 1987.

Winthrop, John. "A Modell of Christian Charity." In *Winthrop Papers*, vol. 2: *1623-1630*. Boston: Massachusetts Historical Society, 1931.

Wood, James E., Jr., ed. *Baptists and the American Experience*. Valley Forge: Judson Press, 1976.

———. *Religion and the State*. Waco, Tex.: Baylor University Press, 1985.

Index